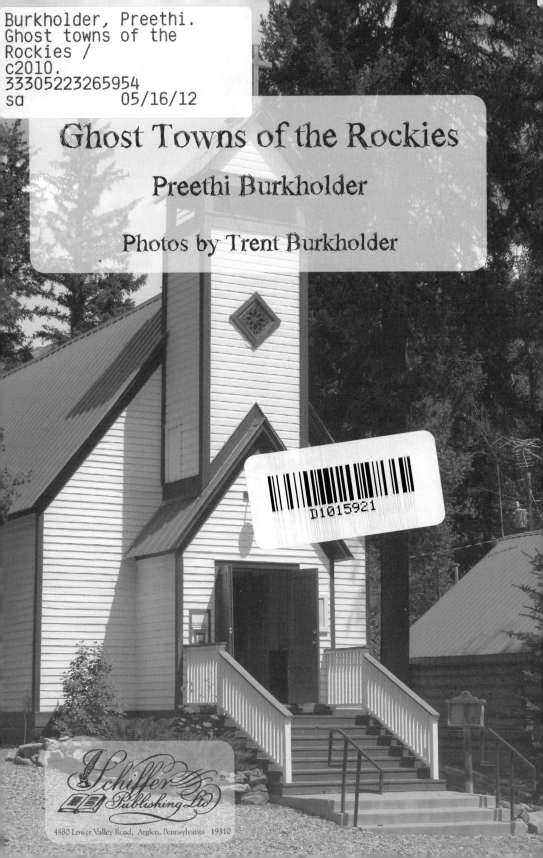

# Ghost Towns of the Rockies

## Preethi Burkholder

### Photos by Trent Burkholder

Schiffer Publishing Ltd

4880 Lower Valley Road, Atglen, Pennsylvania  19310

Copyright © 2010 by Preethi Burkholder
Photographs by Trent Burkholder
Library of Congress Control Number: 2010926738

Designed by "Sue"
Type set in !Sketchy Times/New Baskerville BT

ISBN: 978-0-7643-3569-3
Printed in The United States of America
Text and photos by author unless otherwise noted

Schiffer Books are available at special discounts for bulk purchases for sales
promotions or premiums. Special editions, including personalized covers,
corporate imprints, and excerpts can be created in large quantities for special
needs. For more information contact the publisher:

Published by Schiffer Publishing Ltd.
4880 Lower Valley Road
Atglen, PA 19310
Phone: (610) 593-1777; Fax: (610) 593-2002
E-mail: Info@schifferbooks.com

For the largest selection of fine reference books on this and related
subjects, please visit our web site at **www.schifferbooks.com**
We are always looking for people to write books on new and related
subjects. If you have an idea for a book please
contact us at the above address.

This book may be purchased from the publisher.
Include $5.00 for shipping. Please try your bookstore first.
You may write for a free catalog.

In Europe, Schiffer books are distributed by
Bushwood Books
6 Marksbury Ave.
Kew Gardens
Surrey TW9 4JF England
Phone: 44 (0) 20 8392-8585; Fax: 44 (0) 20 8392-9876
E-mail: info@bushwoodbooks.co.uk
Website: www.bushwoodbooks.co.uk

# Contents

# Dedication

To Every Immigrant Who Left Their Homelands
and Came to America, Searching for a Better Life

# Acknowledgments

Thank you God for giving me the strength,
hope, and motivation to keep getting up
every time I have fallen along life's journey.

# Preface

Ever since I was a little girl, my dream was to come to America. The impression created by the media was that every person who made it to America struck gold. I believed it.

I thought that America was the land of opportunity which would recognize my talents and reward me financially, emotionally, and spiritually. I had visions of it being flooded with money lying on pavements. I thought that I could pick up money if I felt like it or simply walk past it if I already had enough of it.

Consequently, when I came to America at age twenty, I expected the road to finding the money to be an easy one. I thought that all I had to do was put a little bit of effort to reap the gold. I could not have been more wrong.

Some fifteen years later and still counting, I came to the conclusion that finding gold in America is not that easy. Some get rich overnight, others never make it. A handful of immigrants become millionaires within a matter of hours, but that is the rare exception. Some even have to take a couple of notches back from the economical status that they enjoyed in their homelands. Many immigrants struggle to find the American dream. Some never do.

As I wrote this book I realized that it was the same dream that I had in the twenty-first century, that drove people to come to America, in search of silver, gold, and lead in the nineteenth century. They had the same aspirations and dreams that I had. They left their homelands with the expectation that America could offer them something better. Some found it, and some didn't. A handful were sent back to their home lands, but most stayed behind.

As a first generation immigrant, this book strikes close to my heart. I was happy in my country of birth of Sri Lanka and never thought that I would leave my family behind in search of the unknown. Still, I thought America could make me happier. So, I left everything behind, vowing never to look over my shoulder as the decades passed by.

My journey is still continuing in America. Even though I am still searching, what I have gained emotionally in America has been priceless; and that is the freedom to discover my inner self, for me to think for myself as a woman, and for me to keep searching for that "something." I feel that it is this soul searching that drove every individual to travel across the continent and endure the bitter winters in order to strike it big.

In the end, it is all about the journey and less about the final destination. Money is not everything. Some of the historic figures who made millions from gold and silver were miserable during their lifetime trying to cope with all the woes that money brought along with it. The poor miner on the other hand, may have had all the happiness in the world that money could not buy. In the end, the old adage comes true, that money does not buy happiness.

Writing this book has been a healing experience for me. I realize that millions of people have explored America, just like I am doing today. In the eighteenth century people came in wagons to Rocky Mountain mining towns to find gold and silver. The trend still continues three centuries later, not to claim gold and silver, but other riches. People still come from far off lands to America to strike it big; they don't come in wagons, but in airplanes, ships, and a few come walking for hundreds of miles across borders. It is the lure of money that attracts people from all over the world to come to America.

The mining era in the Rockies would have been a fascinating time period to live in. The Rocky mountain states and the West stand out from the rest of the country. While people in the wild west lived under the stars, other parts of the world had innovations going on. Albert Einstein published what he referred to as his "Theory of Relativity." Jazz was hot in New Orleans, and the electric bulb was invented. In Europe, Germany was using helium filled Zeppelins to firebomb historic French cities and World War 1 shook many remote corners. General John Taliaferro Thompson had just invented a hand-held fully automatic weapon that would later be called the "Tommy Gun." Ceylon and India were British colonies, with a prosperous tea exporting trade. However, in out of the way places like Wyoming, Arizona, and New Mexico, the Old West lived on.

In the 1800s, folks in the Rockies were more likely to settle disagreements personally rather than resort to the insular objectivity of the law. Indians were trying to be on the soil that they had inhabited for centuries. The 1880s were the decade of agricultural and pastoral pageants that were never seen again. The cattle economy allowed enormous remittances flowing back to the Eastern city folk who owned the West. The era of the cattle kingdom however, was very brief. Mother Nature took care of it. A terrible vengeance was created upon the cattle by the weather in 1886. Drought and harsh winters could not be organized away. The grass was roasted by unremitting sun; the rains refused to fall; and the cattle died of thirst. Then came the blizzards. There are stories of ranchers driven mad by the sound of their cattle lowing for food. When the winds stopped, cattlemen found thousands of carcasses filling ravines. The dead cattle became natural fertilizer. Indeed, these were hard times for the cattle industry.

The collapse of the bonanza decade was more rapid than its boom and the cattle kingdom did not recover. As the depression diminished the market for beef, many of the great companies went to their creditors, who sold the herds into already flagging markets.

On into the 1930s in the Rocky Mountain landscape. There were still more horses than cars in the borderlands, more deer than registered voters, and more cowboys than tourists. The automobile opened up doors for more people to travel and explore the West. Outside of the trendy city areas, folks still dressed much as their grandparents had. They wore wide brimmed hats and dusty chaps. Self reliance was at an all time high, especially among the men. They continued to believe in hard work. They flourished like cactus in even the harshest environments, generally seeking no one's help but their own. Some were resilient, homesteading land and working on ranches. Some were Mexican or Mexican-American, recent immigrants in search of better paying work. Others were the descendants of families that had already lived here for hundreds of years. Some were Native Americans.

Probably the pivotal event that spelled doom for thousands of miners and people in the Rocky Mountain states was the silver crash of 1893, better known as "the panic of 1893." America's money at the time was based on a "bimetal" standard of gold and silver. However, in 1893, the nation switched to the gold standard. In July 1890, Congress had enacted the Sherman Silver Purchase Act, which required the Treasury Department to buy specific amounts of silver each month at the market price. The principle buyer of the silver was the United States government. The Silver Purchase Act resulted in a rise in silver prices, but supplies increased and overtook demand, and the price fell to 99 cents in 1891 and to 87 cents in 1892. In the spring of 1893, President Grover Cleveland announced that he would repeal the Sherman Act; but it was too late. Silver prices had already plunged. Mines closed overnight.

The demonetization of silver contributed substantially to the panic of 1893 which closed many banks across the country. Silver subsidies helped undermine the nation's economy. With America's entry into World War II, gold mining too, was declared by the government to be a "non-essential" activity and all operations were closed. Almost without warning, it seemed like ore in the ground, bullion at the smelters, and silver at the refineries was worth far less than ever before. The effect was devastating and plunged several Rocky Mountain towns into a depression. In almost every ghost town mentioned in my book, it was the demonetization of silver in 1893 that turned them into dust.

Nothing lasts forever. Every town, city, and culture has its fifteen minutes of fame. Rome was not built in a day; nor did it collapse in a day. This same principle applies for ghost towns. They all had their fifteen minutes of fame, and a lucky few were able to enjoy prosperity for a second and third time around. In many cases however, prosperity was a one-time deal that came and went.

Many of today's ghost towns were prosperous mining camps, boom towns built upon silver and gold. They bloomed briefly, then faded and died. Sometimes they were deserted overnight when the miners left to answer the siren calls of rich strikes elsewhere. More often they died when their veins pinched out, or when underground water flooded their shafts. The miner was gone forever and the few fragile remnants of the town they built disappeared as well.

When I first started to work on *Ghost Towns of the Rockies*, I thought I was going to be working on a book of the past, a topic that was essentially "dead." I thought that my efforts were to create an appreciation for stories from a bygone era that we are not likely to see again. At first glance, a book about ghost towns seems to be about forgotten places. This is far from true. The topic of ghost towns is not a dead one. It is in fact, very current. As Thucydides once said "history repeats itself." The deeper I got into this book, the more I realized that we, in America, were re-living history. America was getting deeper into a depression. In 1893, it was the demonetization of silver. Some 115 years later, a similar economic turbulence was being seen. The gradual demonetization of the dollar was being caused partly by the housing and banking collapse coupled with a sleuth of Ponzi schemes resulting in corporate fraud.

It was around the same time that I was writing this book that the recession started to take its toll. The news started flooding with stories about towns in Florida, California, and the mid-west becoming ghost towns because of the economic strife. Over 700 post offices closed within a short span of three months and major corporations began to shut their doors. The housing market collapsed, with "for sale" signs mushrooming everywhere. Mass migration patterns began to take place, with people moving from towns to cities where they thought they could find jobs, only to find that the competition was too keen, and so they moved back to small towns and started plowing the fields for an income.

Some immigrants who had come to America in search of better pastures were returning to their home countries because of failing to achieve their dreams. The story of an immigrant from Guatemala deliberately committing a crime, in order to get himself deported made headline news. He was not making ends meet in America and could not afford a ticket back home. The only way that he could return to Guatemala was by getting himself behind bars. When all these stories started flooding the media I realized that my book about *Ghost Towns of the Rockies*, was actually about the present, and in a way, about our own future.

Every couple of centuries an economic "cleansing" takes place. This may be man made or natural. Sometimes, the causes for such an economic cleansing may be hidden, almost like a puppeteer behind the curtain.

Some of the towns that are very successful today will wither away into darkness and get claimed by nature or vandalized. New communities are being born every day. The same goes for people. Some of the wealthy millionaires of the old order fall, giving rise to new ones. Horace Tabor of Leadville is a fine example. Once the fifth richest man in the United States who made his millions from the Matchless Mine in Leadville, Tabor lost his fortune in 1893 and died a pauper, shoveling dirt at $0.65 cents a day.

Different people have different ways of describing ghost towns. Basically it can be any town involved in mining or agricultural activity that went through various cycles of boom and bust. They are towns that are important to the history of the United States. Some think that ghost towns are those areas where no people live today; that they are lonely areas where the only inhabitants are a few scattered buildings, shacks, animals, and plenty of trees. Not quite. Some have become vibrant communities even today, maintaining a part of their ghost town history.

In my understanding, a ghost town is one that enjoyed a boom period at one point, and was then abandoned. Many of them remained neglected like Ashcroft, St. Elmo, and Jeffrey City. A few however, experienced a revival and remain vibrant towns even today, like Cheyenne, and Creede. Are there ghosts in ghost towns? Not necessarily, although some visitors *have* said that they hear strange voices and eerie things happenings in some ghost towns. Annabelle in St. Elmo for example is believed to watch over the town. Whether these stories are true or not, I cannot say.

Some folks resent having their present home town considered a ghost town. Being called a ghost town is not to take offense at. It means that the town had a vibrant past which died at one point.

The majority of the ghost towns in this book are being taken over by mother nature and are not bubbling with life any more. At one point, these were vibrant places full of energy, where wives were burning the hearth and looking after the children while their husbands worked in the mines and fields. Today, they are dead towns, with chipmunks and deer crossing through bat-infested cabins.

Some towns examined in this book, hardly have a "ghostly" feel to them. They are functioning and bubbling with life. They almost died, but because of a handful of gentle individuals or because of the town's chance to produce a valuable mineral, got revived again.

Most western ghost towns were once mining towns, built during the booms that began in California in 1849 and continued into the early twentieth century, on the promise of profits to be realized from a region's abundant mineral deposits. As mineral strikes slowed, or natural disasters took place, prospectors and those providing them goods and services such as merchants, saloon owners, bankers, and prostitutes left homes and businesses so abruptly in order to move on to the next strike. As a result of such volatile economic conditions, the towns were often left in a state of suspended animation, with displays still standing in shop windows, bottles and glasses on saloon tables, and the shelves of abandoned cabins lined with pieces of crockery and silver ware. Understanding a book about ghost towns serves as a warning on how quickly the tide can change.

Most treasure tales and lost mine stories are substantially true. Grandpa did bury his money somewhere out behind the barn and a distant uncle may have had a mine somewhere. The older members of the family can remember Grandpa getting gold coins from his cache to pay the mortgage. But after Grandpa died no one knew where his cache was located. These kinds of stories have become today's treasure tales.

The relationship between ghost towns and their inhabitants was a fair weather one. So long as the money was good, they stayed on. When the money ran out, so did the people. Economic collapse was the pervasive reason for every mining town to fall. A hundred years from now, books could be written about our present times, where vibrant cities and towns as we know them now, are likely to be called ghost towns. Detroit is already becoming a ghost city, with the auto industry in a state of collapse.

Covering every single ghost town in the Rocky Mountain States is impossible. There are thousands of them. Some may never even surface in historic records as all the buildings have been destroyed or have been developed by real estate companies. I have selected just a handful.

The towns selected in this book have all had an active history at some point. The majority are linked to mining history. A few have different backgrounds. Topaz, Utah, for example, was an internment camp for Japanese-Americans in 1942, while Jeffrey City, Wyoming, traces its one-time wealth to the atomic bomb.

Readers might begin to feel that every person who entered the town in search of gold, became rich. Wrong. With every mine, only a handful of people got extremely wealthy. The  majority got just chicken feed. The same principle applies today. A handful of CEOs get extremely wealthy, while the thousands of people working for him are barely making ends meet. The roots of capitalism have not changed over the centuries.

For every town that made millions during the mining era, whether it be from silver, gold, zinc, uranium, copper, agriculture, or any other form of industry, there are untold sufferings of many who never got to enjoy them. For one man to get rich, thousands of others had to toil and suffer. Some of them found  happiness along the way.

Visiting ghost towns can help to nurture your own wisdom. They serve as a warning of what can happen during times of economic recession. Prosperity can turn to despair overnight and governments can change the tide according to their agendas. *Ghost Towns of the Rockies* is not about the past; it is about our own present and our future.

Many people are coming to America even today, hoping to find golden opportunities. A few do, but many don't. May America keep its flame burning with visionary leadership and economic prosperity and re-build itself as the land of opportunity. That's the American dream.

# Introduction

# A Miner's Life

Mining is a risky profession, yet, an honorable one. Your father, grandfather, great grandfather, or great-great-father, most likely did some kind of mining, at least for a short while, if not his entire life.

As a tribute to this noble profession, let us remember the forgotten miners and appreciate their triumphs and tragedies. Visiting a ghost town is a means of offering healthy respect to all the miners over the centuries, who risked their lives in order to make ends meet. Some ghost towns are dotted with log cabins once occupied by families, saloons that saw gunfights, hotels that provided lodging, and the Red Light District that housed women of "special virtue." Perhaps the most nostalgic scene in many ghost towns is Boot Hill, or the cemetery. You can spend hours, walking through the cemetery, reading the faded markers of lost miners.

Miners were the lifeblood of every ghost town that made its fortune from silver, gold, coal, natural gas, and other resources. Millions of miners came and went. Each one had a dream; and that was to make a fortune and enjoy life's riches. Only a sliver achieved that dream. Most worked long hours, often spending a bulk of their earnings at the saloon to whisk away their weariness, until they were ready to give it another shot at mining the next morning. Some worked the mines during the day and tilled their fields in the evenings. All they ever saw was darkness. Every night they returned to their hearths, barely having the energy to smile at their wives, who had cooked a simple dinner to fill their empty stomachs. Some, rarely got to see their children grow, as they left their homes at dawn and returned late at night.

Then there were the single, lonely miners, with no one to give them a loving touch. Some of them visited the town brothel and paid the soiled doves for some quick loving, while others searched for a woman to marry. Some of them never found a female partner and got used to the lonely life.

Mining was a complex endeavor, and covered more than going into a shaft and picking at rock with a shovel. It also required a great deal of investment to build underground mining systems.

Candle flames rarely survived the air drafts in a shaft, and most ascents and descents were made in darkness. The miner began his shift crowded together with his partners in the open cages awaiting the stomach-wrenching lurch that started his noisy, clattering descent. When he reached the working level the first task facing the miner "coming on" was mucking. Working with a shovel "off the sheet" he filled a one-ton ore car, then pushed it to the shaft station along the light, eighteen inch rails. Ore cars were first moved manually, or hand trammed.

Inside many mines, there was a canary in a cage. Yes, it was alive and chirping, while the miners went at their picks. No, it was not kept there for company. The canary served a practical purpose. If it died, it was a siren alarm for all the miners to evacuate, because oxygen was running low.

As the mines increased in size and complexity, the miner learned that his health and safety were governed not only by his actions, but more and more by others over whom he had little control.

A miner's life was constantly at risk. Rock dust was not the only problem faced in drilling. Another was the rash of eye injuries from flying rock particles. Of a far more deadly nature was the occasional explosion of the drill itself. Then, there were rattlesnakes.

The newspapers covered the mines primarily from the financially-related standpoints of production, ore reserves and profits. The only other aspect of underground mining to warrant mention in the newspapers, interestingly enough were the macabre accidents that occurred daily. Mine owners rarely cared about a handful of deaths that occurred in the pits, except that it created a temporary slump in the production levels.

The 1880s attitude regarding mine death and injury was quite simple. It was of little real concern to mine owners and supervisors, except that the loss of experienced miners slowed down production. The established legal stand on accidents in the mines and in the United States in general, held that since the worker recognized the risks of the job when he accepted it of his own free will, he alone was responsible for his own health, safety, and life.

Here are a few news excerpts that appeared in the Leadville newspapers between 1879-1880:

> Drowned: John Doonan drowned yesterday in the Cyclops Mine by falling down a shaft into a body of water.
> Down Shaft: Thomas O'Malley meets death at bottom of shaft. Another fatal accident in the mines occurred yesterday when a miner grew dizzy, lost his footing and fell the distance of 170 feet.
> A terrible leap: Thomas Gardner, a miner, fell a distance of 90 feet to his death when a windlass failed.

To get a real glimpse of what the miner would have endured, take a visit to the Mining Museum at Creede, Colorado. It is definitely worth it. The Creede Mining Museum has audio and guided tours of an actual mine, where centuries ago, miners went deep into shafts to extract ore. Remember to wear a jacket while you are down there, as it can get a little cold.

Miners were obligated to pay for their own medical costs out of their daily wages. Some miners who could not afford professional medical attention for an injury simply let their partner perform the required surgery in their cabin. Ugly scars, missing teeth, and poorly set bones, became marks of the working miner. Doctors of widely varying education and competence found fertile fields in mining towns as the mines provided a steady stream of mutilated patients.

Jobs in the mines were hardly desirable. Only males worked the mines, not females. Simple economic need drove men into the mines to collect $3.00 for a ten- or twelve-hour work shift. Considering the nature of the work and the risks involved, that wage was gross underpayment and a major factor making possible the owner's enormous profits. Still, compared with most other labor, the miner seemed to do fairly well. Factory and unskilled laborers in the East, even if they could find a job, received only $1.00 a day. Hardrock mining was certainly not the ideal career opportunity, but it did offer the excitement of the mining camps and a chance for the miner to prospect on his own. The miner did exactly that during his free time, mine prospect holes on abandoned claims and in remote areas still open to claiming. A few became millionaires overnight, by discovering silver and gold.

Miners came from every walk of life, but had one common quality. Most were the malcontents and the wanderers, the adventurers, and those who, after the Civil War and the Indian Wars, found a void within themselves aching to be filled with more excitement. Those established financially, however moderately, or those socially content, were not the ones to spend their last dollars, rushing to a very uncertain future in the Rockies.

Then there were the immigrant miners who came to America from far off lands, hoping to strike it big in the land of opportunity. They came from China, Italy, Germany, and England, leaving their homes in search of the mighty dollar. Some found fortune and lived a luxury life, but most did not.

Ideas of miners and mine owners clashed in every major point; what seemed good for the miner was not good for the owner, and vice versa. The foremost example was the time-honored practice of high grading, the miner's tendency to pocket pieces of particularly rich ore or of metallic gold or silver. High grading originated on the western gold placers, but was difficult because the sluices were in full view of everyone. Laborers were warned that their jobs involved shoveling gravel and nothing more, and that the only hands permitting in the sluice rifles belonged to the claim owner or his trusted manager.

In the early days, miners often risked their lives to ski out for provisions. For example, miners trapped in Independence, Colorado, experienced a harsh winter. They had to dismantle their log cabins and use them as skis to make it to nearby Aspen, in order to avoid death from a cold winter.

People who inhabited mining camps were like gypsies. Miners could not remain content by remaining in one community after the novelty had worn off. They kept hearing of rich mining fields in New Mexico, Colorado, and Arizona. It was their nature to give up what they had and seek something better. Miners were the rolling stones.

Prospectors lured to the West in the hopes of striking it rich settled a thousand towns in the Rocky Mountains. The cry of "Gold!" or "Silver!" or a few flecks of color in a tin cup sent them to remote, often inhospitable locations to search for the precious metals. Close on the heels of the miners were the merchants, the gamblers, the prostitutes, the washerwomen, the capitalists, and the con men. Together, they turned the mining camps into bustling towns where saloons never closed and the safest place for a man to walk after dark was down the middle of the street with a gun in each hand.

This book is for the silent immigrant, who worked diligently, sometimes in fear, sometimes in hope, that with every strike, he might get closer to becoming financially successful. The most genuine tribute that we can give the miner is to read this book and visit a few ghost towns in our lifetime. This will give a glimpse of what their world was like and what miners had to endure in order to build modern day United States of America.

# Section One

# Ghost Towns
# of Colorado

# 1
# Ashcroft

## History

The Ute Indians left only scant evidence of their presence near Ashcroft. Located on the foot of the old Taylor Pass Road, it was settled by miners on their way to Aspen who found silver there and decided to go no further.

Ashcroft was also known as Castle Forks City. T.E. Ashcraft, an early Colorado scout, mountain man, Indian fighter, miner, and jack of all trades, was among the first prospectors to strike pay dirt here in 1879. Therein lies the confusion concerning the name. Many believed the community was named after Ashcraft, and the post office couldn't make out the spelling of the name. Other records show, however, the site was named for the ash trees abounding in the croft here. "Croft" is an Anglo Saxon word meaning small enclosed field.

When prospectors flowed into Castle Creek Valley in the summer of 1880, they brought with them, expectations of how a town should work. After laying the streets out in typical grid pattern, the Ashcroft town site company sold the camp's 864 lots for $5 each. By 1882, lots were selling for between $150-$400.

Ashcroft was platted during the summer of 1880. A post office was established in 1880 and John Nelson was named postmaster.

Ashcroft got its start about the same time as Aspen, and for a while it threatened to outdistance the new community to the east. It was the railroad and the ores that made the difference. At first Ashcroft could only be reached over Taylor Pass, an arduous pass closed most of the winter and dangerous all of the time. To negotiate the pass it was necessary for stage or wagon drivers to disassemble the stage or wagon, and lower or raise it piece by piece over cliff walls as high as forty feet. During these years, Ashcroft was the gateway to the Aspen area and therefore, a more important city than Aspen. In the early days, Ashcroft grew faster than Aspen, at one time reaching a population of 2,000. But Aspen through sheer perseverance and richer strikes, began to take over the limelight.

During the boom, which lasted three years, Ashcroft had a school, several saloons, and many other business enterprises. Ashcroft had five hotels. Four of those, the St. Cloud, the Riverside, the Fifth Avenue, and the Farrell, provided room and board. The Hotel View, which still stands at the south end of town, was never actually a hotel; it was a brothel.

The community had a newspaper, school, jail, doctor, bowling alley, several stores, and many saloons. The town even had a suburb and a cluster of cabins slightly upcreek. When the Independence Pass was completed, nearby Aspen began to grow and Ashcroft began to decline. When the Denver and Rio Grande Railroad arrived in Aspen in 1887, the mountain passes above Ashcroft became

useless. The population which was at least 1,000 in 1883 dwindled to 150 before the turn of the century.

In 1881, a couple of years before his marriage to Baby Doe, Horace Tabor, the mining mogul and his partner Joe W. Smith purchased the Tam O' Shanter silver mining property near Ashcroft. Because it was difficult bringing ore from its elevator of over 13,500 feet, it was not a profitable endeavor for Tabor. Horace and Baby Doe built a house in Ashcroft which was, for a while, a getaway from the gossip of Leadville society about their scandalous marriage. For a few years after their marriage in March 1883, Ashcroft was their "summer retreat." Tabor built a lavish home, paneled with gold encrusted wallpaper for his new bride. Whenever Baby Doe came to town, Tabor declared a twenty-four-hour holiday with free drinks for everybody. Baby Doe was well liked in Ashcroft.

Transportation and communication were the lifeblood of a mining community. For a new camp to survive, it had to overcome isolation, haul supplies into the camps and valuable ore out to the processing plants. Toll roads, toll bridges and stage lines sprang up immediately. By 1881, the Carson Brothers stage line was running on the newly completed road from Ashcroft to Buena Vista with a fare for wagons drawn by two animals set at $2.00. Telegraph lines were also important in order to advertise the success of the mines, attract investors, and promote the camp. Ashcroft's two newspapers the *Journal* and the *Herald* needed the telegraph to get news from the outside world.

Typical of all mining camps, Ashcroft sported its share of saloons. As soon as the first tents sprang up, the saloon keeper was the one to "wet the whistles" of thirsty miners. Ashcroft supported sixteen to twenty saloons in its heyday. Nearly three quarters of the male population was single. Saloons, bars, and men's clubs offered the lonely miner a social diversion.

A well-insulated cabin was essential for the long, cold winters of Ashcroft, which averaged eighteen feet of snow annually. Ashcroft was built on the stage route from Aspen to Crested Butte along an east-west orientation. Cabins used insulation materials such as burlap or newspapers. Both were fire hazards.

Ashcroft was once a rowdy mining center. It was visited by Bob Ford, the man who shot Jesse James.

Yet, even Tabor and all his millions couldn't keep a dead dog alive. Its heyday was short lived.

With Ashcroft's marginal economy, information was the most important commodity. Post master Dan McArthur earned only $1.50 a month, handling an average of 254 pieces of mail.

When the Denver and Rio Grande reached Aspen in 1887, the jig was up with Ashcroft. A few die-hards held out, hoping the railroad would be extended to Ashcroft. It wasn't, and eventually, all the Ashcroftians moved into Aspen, many taking their cabins with them.

Ashcroft faded rapidly. Eclipsed by Aspen's richer mines, lower elevations, and two railroads, Ashcroft's boom quickly faded. By 1884, many people had moved to Aspen.

*Opposite page:*
Ashcroft lies in a stunning location
and has been elegantly restored.

The one-time saloon located right opposite the post office in Ashcroft, Colorado.

One of the general stores in Ashcroft, Colorado.

The Hotel View was never actually a hotel; it was a brothel.

During the years, Ashcroft was uninhabited, it deteriorated rapidly, but in 1970 a joint project was begun between the U.S. Forest Service and the Aspen Historical Society to restore some of the buildings which remain.

## What It Is Like Today

Ashcroft is a beautiful ghost town to visit. There are several cabins, elegantly restored. A nearby river gushes through the town. Ashcroft is located in spectacular surroundings. The vicinity is breathtaking, with the beautiful leaves in an array of colors. The area is great for fishing and hunting. In the winter, the valley above Ashcroft is an excellent cross-country ski area, with groomed trails marked according to difficulty and warming huts with hot beverages for skiers.

## Remaining Buildings

The post office, saloon, Hotel View, which was actually a brothel, are elegantly restored. Walk into one of the miner's cabins and see the utensils, iron beds, and lanterns that they used.

## How To Get There

Located 12 miles south of Aspen via State Highway 82 and Castle Creek Road.

## Juicy Piece of History

One man lived alone in the town for many years, long after everyone else had moved to Aspen. Jack Leahy lived in Ashcroft for fifty-seven years. He offered legal advice, although he never took a bar exam. He was justice of the peace, but never had any cases. Only in Ashcroft could Leahy re-invent himself into a philosopher and a man of the law. Jack Leahy, known as the hermit of Ashcroft, finally moved out 1935, four years before his death. He died of malnutrition in 1939 and was Ashcroft's last permanent resident.

# 2

# Aspen

## History

Aspen owes its origins to silver. In the summer of 1879, four prospectors from Leadville decided to search for silver in Aspen. They found it and the word spread quickly. Winter prevented much prospecting. Among the first to arrive were Clark Wheeler, who would not wait for the snow to melt. Deciding to challenge the mountains in the dead of winter in February 1879, he strapped on snowshoes and trudged over the divide from Leadville. Some people thought he was crazy to risk his life in the cold and snow but Clark Wheeler was a promoter of grand schemes. He wanted to get in on the ground floor of the silver boom.

The new town took shape that summer in 1880. In came the first businesses: a hotel, sawmill, restaurant, law office, saloons, and more. Business people worked out of canvas tents and crude log cabins, and lived literally on top of their businesses. Aspen, like so many mining camps, began as a shabby tent town. Once the mines began to produce, Aspen grew steadily. The Mollie Gibson Mine paid off ten million dollars in dividends after just seven years. The Smuggler Mine for example, produced the largest silver nugget in the world, weighing 2,060 pounds.

Aspen also became a seat of government. As the silver boom gathered its strength in the summer of 1880, Aspen and the two other camps nearby, Ashcroft and Independence, were part of Pitkin County.

Once the railroads came, hundreds of homes were built each year to accommodate an increasing number of new settlers, and because wealth was abundant here, many of these homes were among the finest to be found in the West. Two newspapers, the *Aspen Times* and the *Rocky Mountain Sun* went to press in 1881. Telephone service began in 1885. Soon the town had musicals, dramas, informal dances, and balls.

Until the late 1880s, Aspen's isolation and the lack of rail transportation hindered the development of its silver mines. Due to the town's isolation, ore-freighting costs were high, so Aspen developed slowly.

The pace of Aspen's growth changed in 1882 when Jerome B. Wheeler (no relation to Clark Wheeler) arrived in town. Jerome B. Wheeler moved west in 1883, seeking a better climate for his wife, who suffered from a respiratory illness. A large stockholder in Macy's Department Store in New York, he arrived in the Roaring Fork Valley in 1883. He invested much money into Aspen and encouraged others to do likewise. The first electric tramway ever constructed for mining purposes was built by Wheeler. It carried ore from the Aspen Mine down Aspen Mountain into the valley.

Wheeler played an important role in Aspen. He was influential in extending the Colorado Railroad line into Aspen. He also built the town's first bank and the Hotel Jerome. The Jerome was the finest luxury hotel on the Western Slope. Financed by Jerome B Wheeler, the Opera House was heralded as the second best in the state, second only to the famous Tabor Grand in Denver. The grand opening was Aspen's social event of 1889. Due to the silver crash and the high cost of financing touring companies however, the theater grew dark within five years. Today, the Opera House is owned and funded in part by the City of Aspen.

Aspen grew rapidly in the mid 1880s, much of it attributable to Wheeler's willingness to invest his money in a myriad of enterprises. By 1884, the population was 3,500. Aspen built ten churches during the 1880s. Millionaires built their houses on Hallam Street.

Pioneer Park was built in 1885 by Aspen's first mayor, who was accused of murdering his wife with strychnine. The house was later bought by Walter Paepcke, who founded the Aspen Institute for Humanistic Studies in 1949.

By 1892, Aspen was a bustling city with electric lights and telephone service. Ten passenger trains arrived and departed daily. There were horse-drawn street cars. Aspen had three banks, a hospital, three schools, and even a racetrack.

Because it was a mining town, men dominated Aspen's populace. In 1885, three out of every four residents were male. The majority of the saloons lined Cooper Street. Beer consumption was high. Eventually, Aspen required its own brewery to meet the demand. Crimes, ranging from drunkenness and disorderly behavior to assault and battery resulted in about 100 arrests every month.

Prostitution was common in Aspen. The "sporting" women kept many a miner busy. Business was so good that the city collected $5 a month in taxes from each girl. Part of Durant Street was the Red Light District. Many brothels housed the ladies of the night (and day). The principal form of cultural entertainment was opera. Touring companies from around the country stopped to perform at the magnificent Wheeler Opera House. By 1892, the population soared to 12,000. It had surpassed Leadville to becoming Colorado's leading silver producer.

The silver crash of 1893 had a devastating effect on Aspen. Within one month after the devaluation, all area mines had shut down. Economic strife hit the community. Wheeler lost his house and the Wheeler Opera House after the silver crash and the failure of his bank. In 1912, the opera house burned but was restored later.

By 1930, the population slumped to 700. The glory days of silver were nothing more than a distant memory. Until the 1940s the source of the new bonanza remained elusive. Then Aspen discovered snow. During World War II, ski troops of the 87th Mountain Infantry trained on slopes near Aspen.

# What It Is Like Today

People live in Aspen year round and it has a strong tourist industry. There are summer and winter activities that draw thousands of visitors to the town. The X-Games, skiing, and snowshoeing, are some of the outdoor activities. Aspen today is a world-class ski resort. The Aspen Music Festival takes place in the summer. Another celebrated institution is the Aspen Institute. The International Design Conference is held in the summer.

## Remaining Buildings

St. Mary's Catholic Church, constructed in 1891 at a cost of $18,000, is one of two remaining nineteenth century churches in Aspen. The stained glass windows on the second floor are gothic in design. The Webber Clock built in 1892, where the ISIS Theater stands, was built in 1892. It is a typical example of Victorian commercial architecture.

The *Aspen Times* Building lies on Main Street. Housed in a typical commercial building erected in 1905, the *Aspen Times* is one of the oldest newspapers in Western Colorado. The first issues were printed on a six-ton press freighted over Independence Pass on sledges. *The Times* purchased the present building in 1905. The Pitkin County Courthouse was built 1891 and still stands.

The Wheeler Opera House at 328 E Hyman Street was built in 1889. It reflects the confidence and cultural aspirations that were so evident in many Victorian mining communities before the crash of 1893. The architectural style reflects the way in which the late nineteenth century Victorians revived many of the architectural forms developed in Renaissance Europe.

---

### Juicy Piece of History

Financed by Jerome B. Wheeler, the Hotel Jerome on 320 Main Street has served as the heart and soul of Aspen. Its grand opening took place in 1889. The Jerome had amenities such as indoor plumbing, hot and cold running water, electricity, steam heat, one of Colorado's first elevators, and a paging system. All these helped to justify room rates of $3 and $4 a night, the equivalent of a full day's pay for a miner. Hotel Jerome cost $160,000 to build in 1889 and boasted one of the West's first elevators and a greenhouse to supply fresh vegetables. It opened with a gala Thanksgiving ball that drew guests from New York and Paris.

In the spring of 1893, Aspen's world came crashing down. The effect was devastating. Within a month, all the mines in Aspen had shut down. The mining force plummeted from 2,150 to 150 men. The bank closed and Aspen was in economic ruin. Jerome Wheeler went bankrupt in 1901.

The Jerome's fortunes, however, fluctuated with Aspen's. A mere 25 years after the gala opening, Aspen's population plunged to 500.

The Jerome served more as a boarding house than a hotel. Yet it still provided the community with a place to dine and gather. In 1946, the Jerome was purchased by the Chicago industrialist Walter Paepcke, the father of the Aspen Renaissance.

# 3

# Creede

## History

In 1890, Nicholas Creede (William Harvey), a prospector, stopped for lunch in the mountains close to Creede. While idly poking at the ground, he detected some ore and exclaimed, "Holy Moses, I've struck it rich!" The mine was aptly named, "Holy Moses Mine." Creede's Holy Moses mine launched a rush to the area and within a year had taken $6 million in silver from the hills. In 1882, there were over 8,000 people living in Creede.

Creede grew at an incredible rate in the early 1890s. At one point the population was estimated at growing between 150 to 300 people a day. The town even built a restaurant especially to serve 1,000 people daily. Speculators, miners, gamblers, and parlor girls came on every train to the over-crowded vicinity.

Those first few months of Creede's boom, when more than 10,000 men, women, and children scampered all over the mountains for a rich claim or a place to sleep, were most noted for the underworld characters that came here and found a place to sleep. Creede was a melting pot of strange, different, and interesting people. Soapy Smith, a slick and intelligent con artist, and his gang ruled the city for a while.

Bob Ford walked into town early and announced that he was boss. And he *was*, for a while. Bob Ford, the person who killed Jesse James built a dance hall and saloon called the Exchange. He had a reputation. He gunned down "Mr. Howard," Jesse James. Ford opened up the Exchange, about the biggest saloon and gambling joint in town. Creede, during Bob Ford's reign, got so bad that an official vigilantes committee and a mayor were elected to run the camp. About the first thing the vigilantes did was to run Bob Ford out of town. Then, after much pleading by Ford, the committee relented and allowed Ford to return to town for forty-eight hours to close out his business. Ford was promised protection if he would behave himself. It was during this two-day period that Ed O'Kelley walked into Ford's Exchange and gunned down "that dirty little coward." Bob Ford died.

There were no tears shed over Ford's death, but O'Kelley was almost lynched anyhow for defying the vigilantes committee. He was arrested, received a jury trial, was convicted, imprisoned, and pardoned a few years later.

The Creede underworld financed Ford's funeral. The ceremonies weren't too impressive, but the wake was tremendous. They broke out the whiskey at the burial site on Boot Hill, and began dancing on the grave. The party lasted for days, until the whisky and the women gave out. His burial grave can be visited even today in the Creede Cemetery.

Abandoned rail cars lying opposite the Creede Museum. Silver was transported in these at one point.

Some 5,000 people were here by 1892, 8,000 by the following year, and 10,000 by 1894. Real estate soared and more than a few made a fortune in just buying and selling lots. Guns were a way of life in Creede. The rule was that a man had to start building on the land the same day he got it or he had no claim to it by nightfall. One woman stood by night and day until carpenters finished building her home. Then she turned around and sold it the next week for $10,000.

Contracting the overwhelming underworld were the men of God, who, until the churches were built, preached in saloons, gambling halls, and mines, anywhere a group of man gathered. There is also the story of one itinerant preacher who had his pants stolen shortly after the sermon.

A branch of the Denver & Rio Grande rolled into town in 1891. Creede became county seat of the newly organized Mineral County in 1893.

Creede had more than its share of fires and floods. In 1892, a fire, which started in a saloon, destroyed most of the business district. In 1892, a fire started in a saloon, spread down Creede Avenue, and eventually destroyed most of the business district. The fire and silver crash of 1893 created a mass exodus and spelled the end of the boom.

But Creede has survived all the Bob Fords, Soapy Smiths, fires, and floods and is very much alive today. To date, millions in gold, silver, zinc, and other minerals have been taken from the area.

N.C. Creede who started the town died in Los Angeles in 1897, not so rich and not so happy. In fact, he committed suicide by taking morphine. He had separated from his wife a short time before. His wife wanted to live with him, but he preferred death.

## What It Is Like Today

Creede today is a friendly town, proud of its rich mining heritage. There are people living in the town year round and the population is growing. It hardly seems like a "ghost town," because of its vibrant community. Historic buildings and names from a bygone era mark the quaint seven-block downtown section of Creede's famous silver mining era. The spectacular Pillars of Hercules, volcanic cliffs rising nearly a thousand feet at the edge of town, frame Creede's array of shops, galleries, eateries, lodging, and services. The lakes around Creede are popular for fishing.

Bob Ford's grave lies in Creede. He was shot in his own salon in Creede.

## Remaining Buildings

This town is very much alive and also presents remaining buildings of a once thriving community. Both the Mineral County Courthouse and the Creede Town Hall are located on North Main Street. The cemetery is on the hill and is definitely worth visiting. Remember to visit the grave of Bob Ford, which is a little upwards and separated from the rest of main part of the cemetery.

## How To Get There

Creede is in Mineral County, Colorado, and is in the San Juan Mountain area.

## Juicy Piece of History

Soapy smith ruled Creede for a long time. The infamous Soapy Smith was a late 19th century American confidence man and gambler par excellence. Known as the "king of the frontier confidence men" he was a crime lord who organized a powerful gang in order to assume control of the criminal underworlds in Denver and Creede, between the years 1884 and 1895.

Soapy Smith ran the Creede underworld. He got a cut of every gambling concession in the city. Soapy was named for his special con game. It worked wonders in boomtowns throughout the west. Soapy would sell soap on a street corner, wrapping some of the bars in hundred dollar bills, tens, and twenties. The purchaser was allowed to keep any bill he found around the bar of soap he could buy for as little as five to twenty five dollars. It was a scam.

He was shot dead in a horrific gunfight on July 8, 1898. Four days prior, he had been the man of the hour. He had led Skagway's first Independence Day parade as its grand marshal, and he stood on stage along side Alaska Territorial Governor John Brady. Four days later he died, labeled a criminal outlaw. Soapy Smith was the last of his kind, an old west crime figure who refused to give up the old ways for a constantly changing modernizing nation. His motto was "Get it while the get'in's good." In the days of the old west, no one proved more slippery.

*Opposite page:*
A short drive away from the main part of
Creede reveals a string of abandoned mines.

# 4

# Emma

## History

The town of Emma, was once a busy railroad stop. Robert M. Morrison established a small store on the stage line to Aspen and the town of Emma was born. The Denver & Rio Grande Railroad built the town in 1888 at the intersection of the rails and an older stage road. Following the arrival of the Denver & Rio Grande Railroad, a railroad station, section house, and water tank were rapidly constructed.

Railroad crews named the town for Emma Davis Shehi, an ardent prohibitionist who often cooked for the railroad workers. The stop itself consisted of a small station section house, water tank, post office, and a general store.

A post office was established on February 15, 1888. Emma was named postmistress. In addition to the railroad facilities, there were several cabins.

## What It Is Like Today

Today, Emma is nothing more than several buildings, a house, and a school.

## Remaining Buildings

There is a schoolhouse, a brick commercial buildings and a few other buildings that can be seen on the highway.

## How To Get There

On State Highway 82

---

### Juicy Piece of History

Emma Garrison often cooked for the railroad workers and it was because of her overwhelming generosity that the town was named in her honor.

Later, in 1898, a general store and hotel were constructed of brick by Charles Mather.

# 5

# Independence

## History

Independence Pass was a development of the Lake Creek trail to Aspen, and was originally called Hunters Pass. The route saw a steady stream of wagons and coaches during the early years of the Aspen boom. It was a rugged road. The first wagon over the trail took six weeks. Some wagons didn't make it at all. After the railroads were developed west of the range, Independence Pass fell into disuse.

The Independence Lode was discovered on July 4, 1879, and named for the day on which the find was made. Charles Bennett, leading a party of prospectors into Aspen discovered a lode mine on Independence Day. Independence went through several names. The settlement also changed its name to Mammoth City, and again to Mount Hope, before reverting to Independence once again. One of the longest used and most popular names was Chipeta, for Chief Ouray's wife. A tent city sprung up that summer, and by 1880, there were 300 people living in the camp.

As with most Colorado high mountain towns, the mining in Independence brought investors, quick growth, and just as quickly became a bust. It was a booming mining town in the 1880s. Yet, this town had no great future, as the winters were too difficult. At over 10,900 feet, Independence couldn't last long. Snow from October through May would make sure of it.

Although mining at Independence proved to be short lived, over $190,000 worth of gold was produced between 1881 and 1882. By 1882, the Town of Independence had over forty businesses with three post offices and an estimated population of 1,500. Of the forty businesses, ten were saloons. It was a wild town with the saloons and gambling halls the busiest places in town.

The bust soon followed. In 1883, the production dropped to $2,000. By 1888, only 100 citizens remained in the high mountain town as the gold ran out. As the mines played out, businesses packed up and moved. The old mining town of Independence had a hermit, the Mayor of Independence.

## What It Is Like Today

The thirty-eight-mile Independence Pass spreads through some of the most beautiful country in Colorado. The site where Independence once thrived lies in a beautiful meadow in the high Rocky Mountain country just below Independence Pass. Down by the river, on what was the main street, are several groups of cabins. Independence is a true ghost town, the remains of an early gold camp in a high alpine valley. It is a collection of restored cabins and the remnants of an old saw

Harsh winters in a high elevation made Independence a short-lived town. It lies in a stunning location on a scenic highway, Independence Pass.

mill. The town is visible from the highway. A hike is certainly worth it, though. The road leading to Independence is closed during the winter, but makes a pleasant visit during the summer and fall.

## Remaining Buildings

A few miners' cabins remain. Most of the buildings have markers explaining the building's original function. There are grocery stores, cabins, a sawmill, and some of the saloons when the town was in its heyday.

## How To Get There

Independence is located on Highway 82, twenty six miles East of Aspen.

## Juicy Piece of History

During the winter of 1899 the worst storm in Colorado's history cut off the supply routes to Independence. The remaining miners, who were running out of food, proceeded to dismantle their homes to make seventy-five pairs of skis and escape en masse to nearby Aspen. The town of Independence became a ghost town.

*Opposite page:*
Independence is a restored ghost town. Its ruins can be seen while driving through Independence Pass.

# 6

# Leadville

## History

For a while anyone who was anybody came to, or from, Leadville. Leadville's story starts in 1859 when gold was discovered up the California Gulch. When Leadville was incorporated in January of 1878 about 300 people resided in the snow-covered village. By 1878, Leadville was famous around the world for its overnight millionaires and its streets teeming with gunmen, shady ladies, bunco artists, and gamblers. Men shot each other and died of exposure. Graves were excavated in the frozen ground with dynamite and at least one mine was discovered during a burial. In the overcrowded settlement, miners slept on saloon floors; one fellow made $1,000 a night renting bunks in a large circus tent. Real estate prices skyrocketed, and storekeepers turned scalpers, selling groceries at a 400 percent profit. Even water cost fifty cents a barrel.

By fall, over a thousand people had arrived. They continued to trickle into the area all winter and by the spring of 1879 they were arriving by the hundreds every day. By 1879, the population had reached 18,000. Millionaires were made here overnight. Some made investments of just $37 to make millions in silver mines. Presidents and dignitaries held interest in many of these mines which were producing hundreds of thousands of dollars in income for them every day.

The name Horace Austin Warner Tabor in 1880 is synonymous with silver. Tabor had grown up with Leadville. He came west after marrying Augusta Pierce, the boss's daughter. Tabor, after hearing the get-rich-quick stories, decided his future was in mining. He loaded his family in a wagon, hitched up his oxen, and headed for Denver in 1859, later ending up in Leadville. He was the town's first mayor and leading merchant, having one of the town's two stores and the post office.

Tabor continued to prospect, gambled a bit, and drank with the boys while Augusta and Maxcy his son of twenty, ran the family business. Tabor learned early about "grubstaking," a simple method of keeping your hand in while someone else did the work.

Meyer Guggenheim, known as the father of seven millionaires, is a product of Leadville. Meyer Guggenheim was an emigrant from Switzerland whose American enterprises began with the sale of stove polish, coffee, lye, and lace. From this improbable beginning Meyer and his seven sons were to become leaders in the Leadville mining and the Colorado smelting industries.

For $5,000 Meyer Guggenheim became in 1880, a half owner of the A.Y. and Minnie Mines.

Leadville, Colorado, was a silver mining kingdom at one point. This is where the saga of Horace Tabor took place. Once the fifth richest man in the United States, Tabor was shoveling dirt at $0.65 a day by the time of his death.

Culture came to Leadville with the visit of Oscar Wilde. His visit and lecture of April 14, 1882 received advance publicity, sufficient to pack the Tabor Opera House.

Everything changes. The silver boom didn't last for long. When Congress repealed the Sherman Silver Act, the government was no longer in the market for silver. By June of 1893 the inevitable catastrophe happened. A number of circumstances finally culminated in the price of silver dropping to almost nothing and the "silver crash of '93" as it has been nicknamed brought countless millionaires to their knees.

The Ice Palace was located on Capital Hill. The famed Ice Palace was built in the winter of 1895 and early 1896 when it opened with colorful fanfare to bolster Leadville's morale and relieve the misery that struck, following the 1893 panic.

Ironically, Mother Nature provided the warmest winter the following year. By March 1896, the ice facing of the fabulous structure had melted away leaving only the rough frame foundation.

The Little Jonny was probably Leadville's richest mine. Little Jonny was rare in being both a gold and silver mine in a predominantly silver camp. Its principal owner was John F. Campion (Leadville Johnny) who employed Jim Brown (Molly Brown's husband later) as a superintendent until Brown was clever enough to find a gold belt in the workings of the mine. This was just at the time that the price of silver was falling and the panic of 1893 was casting a pall on the silver camps. In return for this stroke of luck the grateful owners cut Brown in for an eighth share of the mine.

Jim Brown had married Maggie Tobin, an Irish waitress, in 1886. In order to be close the mines that he was managing at the time he had taken her to live in Stumptown. Margaret Tobin Brown was born in Hannibal, Missouri, in 1867. During her younger years she was certain of one thing, the poverty of her family was not the best of all possible worlds. As a teenager she worked as a waitress at a hotel. She always wanted to marry rich.

Jim Brown married her and they moved to Leadville. It wasn't until Maggie's part in the Titanic tragedy that her dreams came true of being accepted to Denver society. She was accepted following her 1912 adventures.

With the silver panic of 1893 Leadville's heyday was over. Leadville declined, with empty streets and silent mines after the turn of the century. Much of the town was torn down for firewood.

# What It Is Like Today

Leadville sits in a high mountain valley surrounded by snow-capped peaks. Located at the foot of two of Colorado's highest peaks, Mt. Elbert and Mt. Massive, Leadville is one of America's last remaining authentic mining towns. It is a vibrant town today. The town has a year-round population and much of the historic character still remains. There are a host of recreational opportunities nearby.

Leadville is a National Historic Landmark District. The small city is comprised of seventy square blocks of Victorian architecture and is adjoined by the twenty-square-mile Leadville mining district, where many old mines and cabins dot the landscape.

The historic Delaware Hotel stands majestically in downtown Leadville, CO.

# Remaining Buildings

There are pleasant surprises around each and every corner. The main avenue includes over fifty significant buildings from the 1870s, including the Tabor Opera House and the Tabor Grand Hotel. The Leadville National Fish Hatchery and the federally-chartered National Mining Hall of Fame and Museum are interesting places to visit, too. The Healy House, built in 1878 serves as a museum of furniture, clothing, pictures and maps of the late 1800s bonanza mining period. The Dexter Cabin, built by James V. Dexter, one of the state's early millionaires, looks like a log cabin from the outside but is finished inside with fine woodwork and hardwood floors.

The Tabor House is worth visiting. After his term, the ex-President and Mrs. Ulysses S. Grant were entertained in this home in 1880. Lying on 116 East 5th Street, it was built in 1877 and was the residence of Horace Tabor and his first wife, Augusta, until 1881.

Named for its stained glass eye, the House with the Eye lies on 127 West 4th Street. There is a small window in an attic roof. It was built in 1879.

Established in 1889 by Congress, the Leadville National Fish Hatchery is the second oldest Federal hatchery operated by the Fish and Wildlife Service of the U.S. Department of the Interior.

The historic Tabor Opera House cost $700,000 to build. With the silver mining crash of 1893, Tabor lost all his fortune.

A saloon dating back to 1879 in Leadville, Colorado.

Opened in 1879, the Tabor Opera House retains the decor of its "last show," when miners spent huge sums to be entertained by New York's celebrated artists. At one point it hosted Houdini, Sousa's Marine Band, Metropolitan Opera, and The Chicago Symphony.

The National Mining Hall of Fame and Museum is the only federally-chartered non-profit mining museum in the nation. Mining's colorful history is showcased.

Visit the Baby Doe Tabor Museum/Cabin and Hoist House at the Matchless Mine. The museum has exhibits of Baby Doe memorabilia.

## How To Get There

Located within easy driving distance from Denver and Colorado Springs, along the Rockies Scenic and Historic Byway. From Twin Lake to Leadville it is 21 miles.

## Juicy Piece of History

Every life has a story and every town has many stories. The story of Horace and Baby Doe Tabor remains one of the fascinating stories of our time and it happened in Leadville.

Horace and Baby Doe Tabor lived as millionaires until the repeal of the Sherman Silver Act in 1893 left them broke in poverty.

The incredible story of rags-to-riches to rags of Horace and Baby Doe Tabor has captured the imagination of the world for decades, and it happened in Leadville.

In 1860, when the California Gulch discovery was made just south of present day Leadville, Horace Tabor and his wife, Augusta, arrived with their son, Maxcy. Horace became the city's first mayor and second postmaster.

In the summer of 1878, Horace Tabor struck it rich after grubstaking two miners on a small claim. Quickly he became the alleged Silver King of Leadville. Tabor also became the acknowledged leader of the silver mining community. He was later to buy, among others, the famous Matchless Mine. He purchased the Matchless Mine in 1879 and for quite some time there was truly no mine that was its "match" as it produced for Tabor up to $2,000 per day in high quality silver ore.

In 1879, Horace Tabor built the Tabor Opera House, which was a legend in its own time. Rapidly replacing the smaller theatres and show houses, it became the most popular spot in town. Horace Tabor's fame grew, and he even served as a senator. In one year, Tabor slept in silk nightshirts with diamond buttons.

In a café, while eating oysters, he met blue-eyed young "Baby Doe" McCourt, a divorced waitress who had come to Leadville to scout quietly for a new and preferably rich mate. Abandoning his wife, Augusta, Tabor began a romance that scandalized Colorado. He married his mistress in 1883, in a wedding in Washington, D.C. attended by President Chester A. Arthur.

His wife left Leadville out of a broken heart and moved to Pasadena, California, where she died on February 1, 1895. Horace and Baby Doe were married.

The newly married couple led the high life, for a while. When the prices of silver fell, Horace Tabor, failing to listen to the advice of others and diversify, faced ruin. In the interim, and adding to the crisis, Tabor had also made a number of unsuccessful, if not unwise, investments in foreign mining ventures that failed. He lost huge amounts of money in Mexico and South America. His reserves were gone, and he and Baby Doe lost everything. But regardless of the now destitute condition of the Tabors, Horace never lost faith in the future, and until his dying day he always found work of some kind, hoping to recapture his lost wealth. At age 65 he was shoveling dirt from Cripple Creek mines a 65 cents per day until he was finally appointed postmaster of Denver just a year before his death. He died on April 10th, 1899, of appendicitis.

On March 7, 1935, Baby Doe Tabor was found dead of a heart attack in her small shack at the famous Matchless Mine. She had, for whatever reason, adopted the storage shack at the Matchless Mine as her living quarters since her husband's death in 1899, thirty-five years earlier. The Matchless Mine had long since been lost to foreclosure and had failed to produce even with several new attempts on the part of the new owners. Her undernourished frozen body was found at the Matchless Mine in 1935.

After her death, seventeen iron trunks that had been placed in storage in Denver were opened, as well as several gunny sacks and four trunks that had been left at the St. Vincent's Hospital in Leadville. All that was left from the Tabor fortune were several bolts of unique, untouched and quite exquisite cloth, several pieces of china, a tea service, and some jewelry, including a diamond and sapphire ring. The famous watch fob and chain given to her husband, Horace Tabor, at the opening of the $700,000 Tabor Opera House was also found.

# 7

# Lenado

## History

Lenado is on a road which was originally a railroad bed. Today, it is a sleepy town, but it had its share of boom times. Silver was discovered in Lanedo in the late 1880s, and from that time, until the passage of the Sherman Silver Act of 1893 spread panic, the town grew to a population of 300.

Lenado was a fairly small camp at the foot of Porphyry Mountain, where the only good mines on Woody Creek were located. The site erupted with activity in the '80s when A.J. Varney located a rich vein of lead and zinc ore. He formed the Varney Tunnel Company and began to bore a tunnel into the mountain. There were several other claims staked, but few amounted to much. Before long, most of the men were working for Varney.

Varney employed 150 men at one time. At its peak the town was inhabited by about 300 people. There was a post office, sawmill, large company boarding house, two saloons, a store, a number of cabins, and a large barn to house the company burros. There was a mercantile store, two saloons, and a post office also.

After the lines closed, the town was almost deserted for twenty years but was revived in the early '90s when a large lead mill was erected here. Then lead prices slumped and the mill closed down. Varney and Company resumed operations in about 1905, reopening the mine and mill, and erecting a sawmill. It wasn't too profitable however, and the company closed down in 1906. The mine was reopened for a short while in 1917 when zinc was needed for the war effort.

World War I brought increased demand for lead and zinc, a demand which lasted only as long as the war.

In 1935, "lumber" Jack Flogus built a sawmill to take advantage of the reserves of Englemann spruce and Douglas fir on nearby Larkspur Mountain and Lenado awoke again. This lasted for forty years until Flogus retired and closed the sawmill, leaving the town quiet once again.

## What It Is Like Today

Today, Lanedo is a sleepy town, surrounded in spectacular beauty. A handful of residents lives here year long.

# Remaining Buildings

There are some abandoned log cabins from the mining days.

# How To Get There

Near Aspen-via Woody Creek Road, approximately ten miles east of Woody Creek Canyon turnoff from State Highway 82. Lenado is an area of spectacular beauty. About forty-five minutes from Aspen.

## Juicy Piece of History

The road to Lenado was rugged. There was talk of improving and extending the trail for a more direct connection to Aspen, but little was done about it. In 1888 the Denver and Rio Grande made plans to run a spur to Lenado. The railroad graded the road bed, but never laid any tracks.

# 8

# Marble

## History

The pure White Colorado "Yule marble" was discovered in 1873 by the geologist Sylvester Richardson along the Crystal River. The town of Marble was established in 1882. There were two camps, Yule Creek and Clarence. Both blossomed in the early 1880s, then grew together to form Marble City, later Marble. The Lead King Mine operated yielding silver, lead, and some gold.

A huge finishing mill, the largest in the world, was built and train tracks were extended to the town to haul away the finished blocks of marble. In 1885, a marble worker opened a quarry to supply stone for the Colorado State Capitol in Denver, but the remote location and the lack of adequate transportation still hampered the commercial development. For years forty-mule-pack trains carried the marble to the railroad. Around 1895, horse-drawn sleighs transported the marble.

The marble was pure white. It was good marble. The trouble encountered at first was transportation. Marble is difficult to handle. The first marble was taken out by wagon over the long, rough road. During the winter it was usually taken out on sleds. This was costly and slow. Nonetheless, a considerable amount was hauled out this way. Finally, in 1905, workers completed a wagon road to help bring the marble to the railroad for shipment.

The original population of Marble was made up of Italians, brought to this country because of their experience in working in the quarries in Italy. Today, wandering through Marble is much like wandering through the ruins of an ancient Roman city.

Marble found a commercial outlet in 1906, when rail services began. The town that grew up here had its streets paved in marble, and local quarries supplied the stone for projects all over the country. In 1906, Colonel Channing F. Meek purchased the Yule quarries and plant and organized the Colorado Yule Marble Company. He created the world's largest marble finishing plant. He also imported expert cutters from Italy, and by 1910, the company was a multi-million dollar business. The Colorado Yule Quarries shipped marble for use in buildings in Denver, San Francisco, Chicago, and other cities. In 1914, over a million dollars worth of marble was used to build the Lincoln Memorial in Washington, D.C.

During the height of production, the company town of Marble had a population of nearly 2,000 people, along with churches, schools, theater, and numerous stores, hotels, and saloons. By 1916, the demand for marble fell, forcing the company to shut down for six years.

Much of the city was destroyed by fire, snow, and rock slides, and even the flood of 1941. Personal disasters did much to bring about Marble's downfall, but the greatest blow was the fall in popularity of genuine marble. The Vermont Marble Company closed down its quarries in 1941. The same year, a cloud-burst up the Crystal River sent a huge tidal wave down the valley and it wiped out most of the city.

By 1942, the Depression, two world wars, and the growing penchant for skyscrapers, for which marble is too heavy, finally conspired to close down the quarry and mill, and the town of marble lapsed into quiet decline.

The Marble Church was built in 1908.

The marble here was said to have been the best and the most plentiful in the world. There is still plenty left. However, people don't use marble as they used to, or if they do, they use a marble substitute. The city of Marble today is fighting off oblivion with a meager tourist trade during the summer months.

## What It Is Like Today

Today, a trip to Marble reveals a quiet little town. There is a quarry above town, as well as an old mill. The Marble Historical Society is housed in a schoolhouse of 1910 and displays artifacts of Marble's past. People come to visit this town and more and more people from around Colorado and elsewhere are choosing Marble to retire. Some come here to get away from it all as it is so remote and off the beaten path. The beauty of the valley remains, and there are a few residents who still live there year round. The remains of the finishing mill can be seen. The main marble quarries can be reached via a four-mile hike.

## Remaining Buildings

The Marble Church, was built in 1908. It stands apart from the main part of the town and lies sleepily, in the interior. A beautiful church indeed. There are historic homes dating back to the 1800s still restored. The Marble Quarry has remains from the past.

## How To Get There

South of Redstone off State Highway 133. Marble is about a one-hour drive from Aspen. Marble is twelve miles further up the Crystal River Valley and off the highway to the east.

## Juicy Piece of History

Marble had three or four newspapers in its day. Perhaps the most important was the *Marble Times*, published from 1892 until the early 1900s. One of the editors was Sylvia Smith, a sharp tongued crusader against many people and things, especially mine owners. She was escorted out of town.

The Tomb of the Unknown Soldier, in Washington D.C., was from Marble. It took 75 workers at the Colorado Yule Marble Company quarry one year to cut the enormous stone required for the Tomb of the Unknown Soldier. The block weighed 56 tons after it was trimmed.

The first piano was brought into Marble in 1889 after a long, difficult trip from the east. The trip didn't do the piano much good; in fact it sounded terrible.

# 9

# Redstone

## History

Tucked beneath red cliffs next to the Crystal River at 7,203 feet, is the tiny community of Redstone. It is known as the "Ruby of the Rockies." Redstone was a fair city built by J.C. Osgood. He reportedly purchased the land around the turn of the century for $100,000. Little is known of Osgood's history. He was born in Brooklyn in 1851. He worked at a number of White collar jobs before making his way to Colorado in 1882. He worked every boom town of his day and must have made a fortune, but nobody's quite sure.

Osgood create the company town of Redstone, which became important in coke production from 1898-1909. John Cleveland Osgood, Chairman of the Colorado Fuel and Iron Company built Redstone as a company town. He created a utopian community. The Tudor style Redstone Inn was constructed as a club house for Osgood's workers and a residence for the unmarried men. Unique, pastel-colored homes were provided for workers with families.

Alongside the Crystal River on 450 acres of land, Osgood constructed his magnificent forty-two-room mansion "Cleveholm." No expense was spared in bringing in the best furnishings from throughout the world. The best Italian artists came to hand-stencil the oak panel walls. Many of the ceilings were done in gold leaf. The library was done in hand-tooled green leather and elephant hide, the music room in green silk brocade, and the dining room in ruby velvet. A huge, hand-cut stone fireplace dominates the drawing room. Even the stables were done in oak. Some of the ceilings were gold leafed. Oak wall panels were stenciled by Italian artists. Elaborate furnishings from throughout the world filled the English Tudor manor.

Strikes by coal miners plus his commitment to improve the steel plant at Pueblo drained his financial resources. Osgood was frustrated. In 1903 he had to turn for money to eastern capitalists John D. Rockefeller and George Gould, who gained control of the steel plant, Redstone, and the mines. Before he left the Colorado Fuel and Iron Company Osgood completed the construction of his magnificent estate, "Cleveholm" on 450 acres of land.

He broke with the company in 1903, and spent the few remaining months of his life in his castle on the Crystal. After he died, his wife, known as "Lady Bountiful" along the Crystal, remarried. The coke ovens began to close in 1908, and the next year the town of Redstone was abandoned.

Some fifty years later, Frank Kistler came into Redstone and wanted to turn Redstone into a ski resort and have several tourist cabins and cottages. He wanted to make it a year-round outdoor wonderland. The plan did not really take off, however.

# What It Is Like Today

The current population is 92. Today, Redstone is a thriving year-round community noted for its arts and specialty shops. Cleveholm, the "Redstone Castle," and the Redstone Inn offer turn-of-the-century lodging. They are also good for special events. In the summer, the town is very much alive. Places to stay include the Red Cliffs Lodge and Crystal Dreams B&B. There is also a small Redstone Museum. The Redstone General Store is open year round. It displays a blend of turn-of-the-century cottages and more substantial Queen Anne houses. Particularly notable are the Tudor-style Redstone Inn and "Cleveholm," the celebrated estate of John C. Osgood. The ovens which were constructed in the late 1890s can be seen today opposite Cleveholm on State Highway 133.

# Remaining Buildings

Today, the Redstone Inn is open for lodging and meals. The Cleveholm Manor operates as a bed and breakfast inn. The church at Redstone has beautiful stained glass windows. The coke ovens are still visible along Highway 133.

# How To Get There

Redstone is a 20 minute drive from Marble, Colorado.

## Juicy Piece of History

John C. Osgood discovered large coal deposits and started the Colorado Fuel Company in 1884. He was an idealist who believed in good wages and working conditions, so he built a most unusual company town; forty pastel cottages, each of a different style and color and a luxurious inn for workers and visitors. The inn at the edge of town was furnished as lavishly, and was intended originally as a club house for the workers. The city itself was a novel experiment in employer-employee relationship. Attractive homes were built for the workers, each one unique and each one in a different color. The best in cultural and educational facilities were provided. The top artists of the day appeared here, and European talent was imported to give the workers instruction in many fields of endeavor.

Osgood had three wives, each of whom created her own share of gossip. His first wife wrote steamy novels about their marriage. The life of his second had been touched with scandal. Because of her generosity however, she was dubbed "Lady Bountiful." Osgood's third wife who eventually sold Cleveholm after his death, was fifty years younger than him.

# 10

# St. Elmo

## (Forest City)

## History

St. Elmo is one of the better preserved ghost towns and certainly worth visiting. St. Elmo was originally settled in 1878 and was made official in 1880 when gold and silver began to bring many people to the area. It was first called Forest City. The post office, however, objected the decision because there were too many towns by that name. The new name of St. Elmo was derived by Griffith Evans, one of the founders, who was reading a romantic nineteenth-century novel by the same name.

Altogether, there were over 150 patented mine claims in the immediate area. The miners worked at several mines throughout the area that were rich in silver, gold, copper, and iron.

In 1881, St. Elmo became a station on the Denver, South Park, and Pacific Railroad line. St. Elmo was the biggest and most colorful city in the district. Although it derived much of its livelihood from the Mary Murphy mine, there were other mines around. It was a supply center and "Saturday Night Town" for the district, a jumping-off place for trips over Tin Cup and Alpine Passes, and it was a main station on the railroad.

Soon, the population reached 2,000 and embraced all the trappings of a single male population with saloons, dance halls, and bawdy houses. Eventually, the area included several merchandise stores, three hotels, five restaurants, two sawmills and a weekly newspaper called the *Mountaineer*. During its boom years, it had a population from 1,500 to 3,000.

Perhaps one family that stands out in the history of St. Elmo is the Stark family. In 1881, Anton Stark, a cattleman, brought a herd to the railroad. Anton was so taken with the town that he and his family quickly took up residence. Anton became a section boss for a local mine. His wife, Anna, ran a general store and the Home Comfort Hotel, which later became home to the post office and telegraph office. They had three children, Tony, Roy, and Annabelle, who worked in the hotel and the store. The survival of the town was largely due to the Stark family who remained the sole year-round residents for many years. Mrs. Stark was a disciplinarian and kept a tight rein over her children. Many considered their hotel to be the cleanest and the best in town.

Fire swept two blocks of the city in 1890. The post office was one of the buildings destroyed. The postmaster was both the hero and the goat in the conflagration. He saved the mail, at the expense of the liquor supply.

St. Elmo was among the stops of Colorado's famous "itinerate preacher," Father Dyer, and of Bishop Macheboeuf. The two men of God preached wherever

St. Elmo is a well restored ghost town lying in a stunning location.

The main street strip of St. Elmo. Visitors have reported ghost sightings of Annabelle, a former inhabitant who is believed to watch over the hotel.

The blacksmith shop and the livery stable in St. Elmo.

they could get a group together, often in saloons or gambling houses. But after the St. Elmo school was built in 1882, church services were held in the school.

In 1926, the railroad tracks were torn up and the railroad grade was used to drive from Nathrop to St. Elmo. But the Stark family stayed, believing that St. Elmo would thrive again, buying up property at tax sales.

For many years, Roy and Tony Stark tried to influence developers in re-opening the mines. It didn't work. Consequently, they turned to tourism, leasing the empty cabins to vacationers and continuing to run the general store. After Anton Stark's death, Anna found it difficult to support the family only through tourism. She sent her daughter Annabelle to work in the telegraph office in a nearby town named Salida.

Annabelle felt a tremendous release. She felt that she had been under her mother's tight rein for so long and that being away would be exhilarating. Apparently not. Before long, she met a young man named Ward, and in 1922, they decided to get married, sending a telegram to her family that they were moving to Trinidad. Though no one seems to know why, the marriage didn't work and just two short years later she returned to St. Elmo, where she spent the rest of her life.

The three Stark children were considered eccentric. Along with their mother, they continued to run the general store and rent cabins to tourists. The town however deteriorated. By 1930, the population of St. Elmo had dwindled down to only seven.

Anna and Roy died in 1934. The only residents left were Annabelle and Tony who lived in the dead town without indoor plumbing or electricity. The locals began to call Annabelle "Dirty Annie" because of her filthy clothing and tangled hair. She was also known to have roamed the old town, with rifle in hand, to protect her property. The store and their personal hygiene were thought to be "sour smelling." They were sent to a mental institution for a while.

However, after just a few weeks, a sympathetic friend convinced the authorities that they were of no harm to anyone and they were released. Tony died a short time later. Annabelle was sent to a nursing home in 1958 where she died in 1960. Their property was left to the friend who had helped them.

Unfortunately on April 15, 2002, a fire in St. Elmo destroyed six of the buildings, including the old Town Hall and Jail and the Stark family dwellings. The town officially died on September 30, 1952, when the post office closed.

# What It Is Like Today

Much of the old main street is still intact, including the Stark Store and other false-fronted business houses that once did a thriving business. This is a beautiful ghost town in a stunning location. There are three year-round residents living here.

# Remaining Buildings

St. Elmo today has numerous structures that have been preserved and are all privately owned. The remaining structures include a general merchandise store, which still operates from May through October, a church, a school building, and many other business structures and cabins.

# How To Get There

To get to St. Elmo, from Buena Vista, take US 285 south to Nathrop, and then County Road 162 west for approximately 16 miles to St. Elmo.

## Juicy Piece of History

Annabelle Stark was a long-time resident of St. Elmo. According to local legend, perhaps at least one of them, Annabelle Stark still keeps a ghostly watch over the town.

Shortly after Annabelle's death, the friend's grandchildren were said to have been playing in a room of the hotel, when suddenly all the doors in the room slammed shut and the temperature dropped nearly twenty degrees. The terrified children refused to play in the hotel again.

Another one of the grandchildren decided to start cleaning out the hotel rooms, making minor repairs, and washing down the walls and floors. After cleaning up for the day, she put away their tools and cleaning supplies, only to find them in the middle of the floor when they returned the next day. After this continued to occur, she placed the items in a padlocked closet. Eerily enough, the tools were in the middle of the floor when they came back the next day.

The legend of Annabelle's ghost lives on. Some believe that Annabelle continues to protect her property and is holding on to it.

# 11

# Silver Plume

## History

Silver Plume is a very small, old rural mining town dating from the Colorado gold and silver rush of the last four decades of the nineteenth century. Although gold was the original metal sought in the Silver Plume area, by about 1864, someone recognized that the grayish rock everyone had been kicking around and cursing was in fact silver ore, and the boom era for Silver Plume began.

The story goes that Own Feenan discovered the Pelican lode way back in 1868. He didn't patent the claim and kept it a secret. But a few months later he became deathly ill, and, on what he thought was his deathbed, he told two friends of his rich strike a few miles above Georgetown. In 1871, when Feenan was able to climb out of his "death-bed" and return to work, he found his claim was working full force and a camp had arisen nearby. The camp of course, was Silver Plume. Feenan's "friends" had taken over the Pelican and Feenan had been cut out entirely.

Silver Plume blossomed in the late 1860s and early 1870s. It developed as a miner's town. It attracted low and average income workers and their families.

Silver Plume was incorporated in 1880 at which time its population was near 1,000. The community had a Catholic Church. A number of wood-frame businesses were densely packed into Silver Plume's commercial district. Silver Plume had its own newspaper called "The Coloradoan." There were groceries, meat markets, dry good stores, laundries, boarding houses, billiard houses, and many saloons, several of which lined Main Street.

In addition to the millions in silver, gold, lead, zinc, and copper mined here, high-quality granite was quarried near Silver Plume. The Pelican mine produced large amounts of ore. A neighboring mine, the Dive, was so close that the owners of the mines fought daily about each other encroaching on "their" vein underground. The fortune hunters and miners came from several European countries as well as the east and mid-west of the United States. For a time Silver Plume was a very cosmopolitan, multi-cultural, and multi-lingual town.

The Pelican and the Dive were the two big mines of Silver Plume. The two apparently tapped the same vein. Therein was the problem. The early history of Silver Plume is rife with the squabbles between the two mines. At one time there were more than twenty suits and counter suits pending between the two mining companies. It almost ended in a shooting war. In fact, a man called Snider, who was owner of the Pelican, was shot and killed by a Dive employee in 1875. In the courtroom, the judge was forced to check the guns of all the participants and the judge himself, kept a gun handy on his bench.

The Pelican finally won out, but the Dive had the last word. Before ending work on the vein, miners in a sad procession came out of the Dive carrying six coffins, said to contain the bodies of Dive's miners killed in a mine accident. The coffins were particularly heavy. They contained high grade ore.

Hamill eventually took ownership of the Pelican. He purchased the Dive property for $50,000. A short time later, he sold the Pelican-Dive for five million dollars and became the richest man in the region.

The town was menaced by fire on numerous occasions. In November 1884 a fire broke out during the night in a saloon on the east end of Main Street. It burnt wood frame buildings of Silver Plume's commercial district. The citizens worked together, to rebuild their town.

Eugene Morgenthau lost his dry good store during the fire of 1884. By the following year he had constructed a large new brick building and had resumed business. Other citizens pitched in as well, and within a few short months, much of the downtown area had been rebuilt.

It was a bustling city during the 1870s when more than 2,000 people lived there. There was a theater, two churches, a schoolhouse, post office, and several stores.

In 1877, the railroad came to town.

When silver mining declined after 1893, to be replaced briefly by lead mining to support the WWI war effort, Silver Plume declined except for tourism inspired by the Argentine Central Railroad and by the first passenger tramway in the nation. The famous Georgetown Loop was constructed nearby, lending importance to Silver Plume. The Sunrise Peak Aerial Tramway began operation in 1907 with twenty-six gondola cars that carried sightseers 2,000 feet up Pendleton Mountain.

The town's further recovery depended on commercial skiing after WWII, largely thanks to veterans of the 10th Mountain Division. Since then people have continued to migrate to Silver Plume. From the 1960s to the present, the recovery of Silver Plume has depended on the migration into the mountains of folks from urban and rural flatlands in Colorado and elsewhere around the nation.

Mining has continued off and on through the years. Part of the town was razed when Interstate 70 cut its path through the valley.

# What It Is Like Today

There are a few residents living in Silver Plume today. The community is host to thousands of tourists each year. Silver Plume looks much as it did a century ago. The train ride around the Georgetown Loop is particularly fun. There are gift shops, residential homes, restaurants, and a museum in Silver Plume.

# Remaining Buildings

The buildings that are left, many of which are occupied, give a representative picture of a typical early-day mining town in Colorado. Mining is still carried nearby. There are historic homes, the old train station, a museum, and many historic buildings. Vehicles can be driven right up to the mine shaft on the hill. A short walk gets the visitor closer to the mine shaft. The mine up the hill in Silver plume is definitely not to be missed. There is an interesting cemetery on the side of the mountain.

## How To Get There

Silver Plume is 35 miles west of Metro Denver. It lies 2 miles west of Georgetown on I-70.

## Juicy Piece of History

Close to Silver Plume lies a monument which was erected in memory of Clifford Griffin who died by his own hand in June 1887. According to legend his fiancé died on the eve of their wedding, and the young Englishman came to Colorado in order to take up mining and forget the past. He discovered the Seven-Thirty Mine on Columbia Mountain and built a cabin at the site. Many evenings the lonely and grieving miner would play his violin in front of his cabin, and his music would echo through the gulch. The bottle of whisky accompanied the violin. Townsfolk would come outdoors each night to listen to him play. One day, as the last note rang out, so did a gunshot. He left a note requesting that he be buried at the site, then took his own life. Clifford Griffin's request was granted.

# 12
# Summitville

## History

Summitville is located in the San Juan Mountains. The town sits at about 11,800 feet and was first mined in about 1870. Early prospectors, led by James and William Wightman, discovered gold near here in 1870, attracting hundreds of fortune seekers. But the prospectors soon drifted away. The Wightman Brothers stayed on, however, and had some ore assayed in Denver. The report was good and another boom began.

Soon there were at least fourteen saloons operating in town. More than $7million in gold was taken out of the timberline mines of Summitville, once the highest of Colorado's major gold camps. Summitville had three booms. The biggest boom of them all was the first one.

At its height, Summitville in 1882 had a population of 1,500, with nearly two thirds working in the mines and mills. To help its miners pass the long winter evenings, one company built a pool hall above its corporate offices and pool sharks from all over the state traveled to Summitville to match their skills against the miners.

The nearby city of Del Norte was important to the history of Summitville. Del Norte was an important shipping point, stagecoach junction, and supply center.

There were several hotels, a newspaper called the *Summitville Nugget*, many stores, saloons, and nine mills to process ore from the mines.

Two of the mines, Little Ida and Little Annie, made a fortune for Tom Bowen. Tom Bowen was a leading figure in early Colorado. He was a former governor of Idaho Territory, and a carpetbagger in Arkansas, before coming to Colorado. He bummed around Colorado boom towns, practicing law and gambling. Finally, he was elected district judge in the San Juans. About the same time he struck it rich on the Little Ida. It made millions for him. He accumulated one of the biggest fortunes in southern Colorado. And like other Carbonate kings, he turned to politics. Once a friend and poker playing crony of H.A.W. Tabor, he defeated the Leadville King in a bitter battle for the GOP senate nomination.

In 1885, the Little Annie announced that it could not meet its payroll. The silver panic of 1893 drove many residents away. The other mines too, appeared to be played out, and by 1889, there were only 25 residents in Summitville. It did reopen for mining several times. The town was revived in 1935 when some of the mines were reopened. The town produced a lot of copper during World War II. Finally, a toxic spill, potassium cyanide, in the early 1990s ended the mining. Now it is the site of an environmental cleanup.

## What It Is Like Today

Today there are just a few buildings still standing.

## Remaining Buildings

A few cabins and abandoned structures remain.

## How To Get There

Near Bennett Peak, in the San Juan Mountains.

## Juicy Piece of History

Gold was discovered in Summitville in 1870 when John Esmund, a rancher found a ledge he claimed was nearly half gold. Each summer he worked the site, extracting an abundance of rich ore, but never did the necessary work to prove up his claim. He returned in the spring of 1873 to find that his claim had been jumped. Others were working his mine. Alas, Esmund had failed to do the necessary paperwork to establish his claim. The Little Annie became the best producer in the area. Although he was discouraged Esmund knew there was much more gold in the area. He moved around the slope and made two new strikes. Not wanting to burn his fingers twice, he did the proper paperwork on these claims.

# 13
# Tarryall

## History

Tarryall was also known as Whiskey Hole. Gold "as big as watermelon seeds" was discovered along Tarryall Creek in July 1859. The city was platted in 1861, and for a very short period was the county seat of Park County. Enough people managed to stay on at Tarryall to found a city, laid out in 1861. John Parsons set up a private mint and turned out $2.50 and $5.00 gold pieces.

The several hundred inhabitants quickly gained a reputation for being inhospitable and of hogging all the best sites. Those who arrived later left in disgust, dubbing the camp "Graball." They say everybody in Tarryall was a whiskey drinker. It is probably because there were many more saloons than normal for a town of its size. Whiskey Hole was a placer claim open to miners low on funds. During the boom days the claim was set aside by 150 miners. When anyone desired a drink and had no funds with which to quench his thirst, he could pan enough gold out of the hole to pay for the liquor.

One newspaper, the *Puma Ledger* told the outside world about life in the new camp. Two sawmills were kept busy turning out rough planks and finished lumber for the growing construction demands at the town. Five saloons also enjoyed a flourishing business. There was a general merchandise, a hardware store, and a meat market. Lodging houses did a good business and there was also a dance hall which was never in want of customers.

By 1896, the Tarryall post office had been established to better serve the 300 people that had settled there. When 1897 rolled around, this number had gone up to 1,000. In 1897, an estimated 50 newcomers poured into the camp daily that year. A daily stagecoach brought in both passengers and mail from Lake George, 13 miles to the south.

However, the "watermelon seeds" soon gave out. Many residents left. The population dwindled as the mineral discoveries proved to be much smaller than first thought. Eventually, gold became scarce and the miners moved on. Tarryall was deserted by 1875.

## What It Is Like Today

Some of the ruins are still visible.

## Remaining Buildings

The old school building, many log homes, and all kinds of mining history.

## How To Get There

From Lake George, go west 1.2 miles, turn right on CR-77 and go 12.0 miles. It is 2 miles North of Como on County Road 33.

### Juicy Piece of History

Tarryall was first called Puma City and came around in 1896. It was also the site of a gold rush. Within its first year, it reached a peak population of about a thousand residents. The Tarryall Post Office soon opened to serve the town.

Because the climate was relatively mild here, people remained at the site all year and the mines stayed open through the winter.

When the prospectors arrived here in 1859 they found the ruins of a few log cabins, believed to have been those of miners killed by the Indians as much as ten years before. The '59ers, perhaps drawn by the old cabins, panned gold "as big as watermelon seeds" in the creek here. Impressed with their find and feeling magnanimous about it all, they said "let us tarry all and share the wealth of the area." A camp was established.

Their invitation was carried far and wide. Before long fortune hunters were flocking here by the hundreds. But instead of the hospitality they expected, they found all the best sites staked out and the welcome a cold one indeed.

In disgust they named the camp "Grab all" and rushed on to locate their own camps and claims.

# 14
# Tincup

## History

In 1860, Jim Taylor and a group of prospectors were first in the vicinity of what was to become Tin Cup. They crossed the continental Divide and pitched camp. That night, their horses broke loose and wandered off. The following morning, they followed the horse tracks to Willow Creek and found their horses. One of the prospectors knelt beside a stream to scoop a drink of water. The creek bed looked promising so he scooped up some gravel in his tin cup. Mixed with the cold liquid were flakes of gold.

Despite these indications of mineral wealth, the area was not settled for a while. The Civil War curtailed mining activities throughout Colorado. Nothing much happened in the region until the 1870s when strikes were made. The first permanent cabin at Tin Cup was built in 1877.

By 1882, Tin Cup was the biggest silver producer in the Gunnison area and the population soared to 6,000. The booming tent and cabin community became known as Virginia City. This started the big debate. Many thought this was a unique camp in itself, and deserved a unique name; Tin Cup, for example. But soon the residents thought a dignified name would be more appropriate. The post office was rooting for this latter group, as it had enough Virginia Cities as it was. The Tin cup movement won out.

Tin Cup had its ups and downs. It was once a bustling, prosperous city, albeit more rowdy than the average. The underworld element actually ruled the town. There never really was any law. Every time an honest sheriff would arrive, he would be told what to do by the leaders of the underworld. If he didn't comply, he was killed. In a macabre way, the cemetery at Tin Cup got filled with honest sheriffs and other good people who did not comply with the underworld's demands.

Tin Cup had several hotels and boarding houses. The town had two banks. One was called the Bank of Tin Cup. It also had a general supply and grocery, meat market, boot and saddle shop, livery stable, schoolhouse, post office, jailhouse, telegraph office, and more. The newspaper called the *Tin Cup Record* was established in 1881.

Tin Cup was one of the wildest towns in Colorado, and had a reputation for being so. During the boom years, twenty-six saloons and gambling houses operated night and day. Parlor girls were quick to fleece a miner of his gold dust. During the lively boom years of the early 1880s, parlor houses were located on the South end of Grand Avenue.

At its peak, there was said to be about 2,000 people here, and shortly after that, the population dwindled. By 1884, the boom was over. Still, Tin Cup remained an active town for years. In the 1890s, it got telephones. Fire hydrants were installed in 1891.

As mining activity declined, many of the parlor house girls moved from Tin Cup. Those who remained moved into the alley behind Washington Avenue and became known locally as the "alley girls." A story is told about one of Madam Sal's girls. Sal was a madam who kept a very tight rein on her girls. One of her girls named "Oh be joyful" fell in love and wanted to get married, but Sal wouldn't release her from her contract. Late one night, the firehouse ladder mysteriously disappeared. It was found the next morning propped at "Oh be joyful's window. She had been whisked away to a quick wedding.

Tin Cup never had a church. On those occasions when an itinerant preacher came to town, services were held in the schoolhouse. Tin Cup was such a rowdy place that no preacher was ever encouraged to establish a permanent church.

William Kreutzer became one of the first forest rangers in the United States. His residence, which was also his headquarters, is presently the Tin Cup Store on Grande Avenue.

Each year, part of September was spent gathering firewood and canning goods for the long and hard winter. Temperatures sometimes dropped to 45 degrees below zero. Stagecoaches, wagons, and carriages came to a halt through much of the winter.

Tin Cup has a unique cemetery. The graveyard is called "The Cemetery of Four Knolls." There are four sections, each on a separate knoll. Protestants are buried in the largest knoll. There is also one for Catholics and another for Jews. The fourth and highest knoll is called Boot Hill, the resting place for men gunned down during Tin Cup's wilder days. The fourth was the most active in the early days.

Winter burials usually took place in Buena Vista, for the ground at Tin Cup was too frozen for digging. Funerals were allowed to travel toll free over Cottonwood Pass. Mourners paid toll on their return.

Tin Cup weathered the panic of 1893. And just when things were getting slow again, another boom came in 1902 and 2,000 fortune hunters rushed back to Tin Cup. Finally things began to quiet down for good. By 1912, Tin Cup's days as a mining center were over.

## What It Is Like Today

Tin Cup is located at the south edge of Taylor Park. It looks out at some of the most beautiful countryside in Colorado—pine-covered hills and snow-clad peaks. The Town Hall and many cabins remain, and look much as they once did. Tin Cup today is a prosperous little summer town with a number of log houses, a pretty white church or community center and a general store that sells tin cups. There is a thriving summer community with people who live here and a few who stay all year long.

## Remaining Buildings

There are only a couple businesses in Tin Cup, a small store/gift shop in the middle of town, and Frenchy's, a small log cabin restaurant. There is a historic building that is also the meeting place for Tin Cup's town government and other community events. The cemetery is an interesting place to visit.

# How To Get There

Tin Cup lies 43 miles northeast of Gunnison via State Highway 135, and Forest Routes 742 and 765. The other route is 26 miles north of Pitkin via Forest Route 765.

## Juicy Piece of History

In 1880, the year the rush to Tin Cup really began, the underworld staffed the city offices with their own men, and they told the sheriff that the first man he arrested, other than those specified, would be his last. He only lasted a few months. Harry Rivers became marshal in 1882. An honest man, Rivers, too, soon discovered that honesty was not the best policy in Tin Cup. He was shot and killed by Charles La Tourette, a tough underworld leader. The next marshal committed suicide. That's how things were in Tin Cup. But it did give color to the Tin Cup cemetery.

The story is told about the conversion of Jack Ward. He was about the roughest, toughest, drunk. He used to come to town just to get drunk and pick a fight. He got in more gun battles than just about anyone. Ward ended up in jail. Somehow, during the experience of sitting in jail, old jack found religion. He reformed. Next time he was heard from, was from the pulpit in Glenwood Springs, preaching hell-fire and damnation against gamblers and other rowdy-like characters.

Kate Fisher was a former slave who arrived in Tin Cup in 1880. She operated a boarding house and her fine cooking was renowned throughout the mining community. She was successful, and loved by the townspeople until her death in 1902.

In 1905 it was announced that a horseless carriage, an automobile, was coming to Tin Cup. This was quite an occasion, considering the remote isolation of the community. Well, it didn't arrive but people continued to wait. Finally, everyone heard the engine, and amid much celebration the automobile chugged into Tin Cup. There was an explanation for its delay. The automobile couldn't negotiate the high altitude of Cumberland Pass, so a team of horses had to pull it over the pass to within two miles of Tin Cup where the horses were unhitched and the motor cranked. The horseless carriage was only horseless for a short portion of the trip.

In the 1950s Tin Cup had a curious revival. Denver radio personality Pete Smythe hosted a morning show that he claimed originated from a general store in East Tin Cup, Colorado. The program sent hundreds of listener to visit the mountain community.

# 15

# Turrett

## History

Nestled among the castle-like rock formations at an elevation of only 8,600 feet, it wasn't just gold fever that drew settlers to Turret. It was the beautiful setting. Turrett was a gold camp that was discovered in 1897.

Only a few weeks after the first discoveries, a hundred people were living in tents and shacks and a few log cabins. More arrived every week. By 1898, there were enough miners, families, and merchants living in the area that Pete Schlosser and others filed a plat with the courthouse for the Turret town site.

The post office was established on February 20th, 1898. It had a peak population of about 400. There was a two-story hotel complete with a balcony and wallpapered interior, post office, schoolhouse, general merchandise store, saloon, and a butcher shop. Twice each week a stagecoach arrived from Salida. A newspaper, *Gold Belt*, was published for a short time.

The gold bug played out almost immediately. A flood in 1901 destroyed much of the railroad line and was never replaced. The loss of the railroad was most unfortunate for the many mines that were now operating in the Turret Mining District. Although gold, silver, and copper were found in abundance, it was mostly low grade ore that was too expensive to ship out without a railroad.

Although some mining was done for about twenty years, the real boom lasted for about five years, from 1888 through 1902. After that, the population declined rapidly. Although the big bonanza strike was expected with each turn of the shovel, it never fully materialized in the Turret Mountain Mining District. However, Turret was a pleasant community, in a beautiful location and continued to grow. The *Denver Times* reported optimistically in 1901 "that there has been an inquiry for Turrett city lots for business purposes in anticipation of a coming boom." Turret hung on for a number of years, but the boom never came.

May 1, 1939 was a grieving day for Turret residents. Pete Schlosser died at age 74. Pete had been the Turret Postmaster and the U.S. Postal Service decided to discontinue mail service to Turret and declare it an official ghost town on Pete's birthday, November 12, 1939.

## What It Is Like Today

The road into Turret transverses the main street upon which most of the buildings are located. A few structures still stand in various states of dilapidation. On a small knoll overlooking the town lies the cemetery.

## Remaining Buildings

About a dozen buildings are still standing. There is also a mine.

## How To Get There

Turret is located in a beautiful setting about 12 miles of Salida.

---

### Juicy Piece of History

Pete G. Scholsser of Illinois, the Father of Turrett, claimed to be the first man to eat tomatoes and thus prove they were non-poisonous.

Some families moved into Turret during the depression. These "squatters" lived in the abandoned houses, cabins, and buildings. They planted gardens along the creek. A few "smelted" out a little gold which could be sold to the government for cold hard cash.

---

# 16

# Twin Lakes

## History

Twin Lakes took over from another important town of earlier days, Dayton. Just a short distance from Dayton, the Ryan House was constructed in 1863. It is the oldest stagecoach stop in Colorado. Dayton, which was the county seat for almost two years, eventually phased into the area around the Ryan House to become the resort town of Twin Lakes. It is believed that what was left of the city of Dayton was fast absorbed into fast-growing Twin Lakes. Dayton was last heard of in 1881.

The aptly named town of Twin Lakes lies adjacent to two natural lakes at the foot of Mt. Elbert. Twin Lakes was a mining camp but its spectacular setting and good fishing made it a popular resort. It was once a transportation hub for the mining centers of Leadville and Aspen. Everybody who was anybody in Leadville had a home here and most were of the lavish and palatial variety. With the discovery of rich mines at Leadville and Aspen, Twin Lakes, located on the road between the two camps, became a crowded resort.

Concord stages made the regular run from Leadville to Twin Lakes. Passengers traveling to the boom town of Aspen would transfer to a canvas-top stage for the grueling run over Independence Pass, known then as Hunter's Pass. The stage coach ran through Twin Lakes one block north of present Highway 82. During the Aspen boom and before the railroad got to that side of the divide, a constant stream of stages and freighter wagons rolled over long and grueling Independence Pass. Concord stages would roar down to Twin Lakes from Leadville. At Twin Lakes the passengers and baggage would be transferred to canvas-top stages from the long haul over the pass.

Twin Lakes got its official start in 1879. By 1883, it had six hotels, several lodges, and the lakes were surrounded by scores of homes and cottages. Some buildings were even built between the lakes.

One of the biggest boosters of Twin Lakes was John Campion. Old John took a fortune out of his Leadville mine and put some $125,000 of it into a palatial home in Twin Lakes. Campion built the house for his bride on the lake, with a bluegrass lawn for the peacocks, a kennel of dogs and a tally-ho to transport guests. While the lodge was under construction, he and his bride honeymooned in Europe, picking up the best furnishing the continent had to offer. After Campion sold out, his lodge was turned into a hotel called the "Campion Hotel." It operated for many years.

Campion talked many of the other carbonate kings and several state big wigs into building summer lodges at Twin Lakes. And some of the big names of the day were guests at the Campion lodge. During its peak years Twin Lakes had a population of 200.

Twin Lakes was once the playground for the rich. Today it is a sleepy town lying in a sleepy location.

The lakes were more nearly twins in those days. But about 1880, a company came along and put in a dam that almost joined the lakes. The company was forced to tear down the dam. Later, however, the Twin Lakes Reservoir Company gained control of the lakes and put in a dam, that could lower or raise the water at will. This time the company did it legally. In disgust, Campion and many others moved away. Twin Lakes has never been the same since.

# What It Is Like Today

Twin Lakes is now a sleepy little summer resort. Viewing the lakes and passing through the little village on the west side of the lakes, travelers wouldn't think the site had a fabulous past. Many old buildings remain in Twin Lakes. There is a gift shop, a general store, cabins for lodging, and houses where people live year round. It is a tourist destination in the summer surrounded in spectacular beauty.

# Remaining Buildings

The Ryan House, constructed of logs, has been renovated and now is an attractive house adorned with white shutters. There is a hotel, a few cabins, an old school, a visitor center, and a combination store and service station. There are some new homes that have sprung in between. The Interlaken lies across the lakes and can be seen from the Highway.

# How To Get There

On Highway 82, 21 miles southwest of Leadville via U.S. Highway 24 and State Highway 82.

An old, restored cabin in Twin Lakes.

# Juicy Piece of History

Some say gondolas actually cruised over the lakes. Others say they were just talking about it. A story is told of the time gondolas were planned. The promoters weren't sure of the number to purchase. They put the question to John Morrissey, an ignorant man, and a get-rich-quick millionaire by the Leadville boom. Morrissey told the promoters the number of gondolas to buy wasn't a problem at all. "Just get a couple and let 'em breed," he said.

A leading hotel in the 1800s was the Interlaken (German for between the lakes) and was situated, strangely enough, between the twin lakes. It had a large dance pavilion and many amusement facilities, including ice skating in the winter. The Historic Interlaken Resort and Dexter House, which was a private residence of the owner of the resort, are located on the south side of Twin Lakes and can be seen faintly from the highway. From the village of Twin Lakes, people would usually travel on a boat across the lake to reach the resort.

The Interlaken was expensive, with rooms renting for as much as four dollars per day. The Interlaken boasted the "best cuisine in the country."

The Interlaken was the most popular of several hotels and drew so many guests that one entrepreneur built a steamboat to take them on cruises. While the Interlaken was ostensibly a rustic log hotel, its guests lived in luxury with a paneled dining room, gaming hall, ballroom, and indoor privy. "It is the most charming summer resort in Colorado," wrote George A. Crofutt in 1885. Resort activities were not limited to summer. In winter there were sleigh rides and skating parties.

Today, Interlaken is shut, its windows sealed with wooden bars, and lies abandoned across the lakes. It is a white building with the name "Interlaken" written in Red, which can be seen from the highway. For a closer look, a boat ride is required.

# 17

# Victor

## History

Spanish explorers had searched the Colorado Rockies for the "City of Gold." They never found it. They just didn't stick long enough. Victor was Colorado's "City of Gold." Victor was built on gold ore. The "City of Mines" is located at nearly 10,000 feet on the southwestern side of Pikes Peak, Colorado.

Victor was where the miners lived. It was a working man's town and lacked the sophistication of its bigger "sister-city," Cripple Creek. Victor bloomed just about the same time as Cripple Creek and since many of the richer mines were in Victor, the city rivaled Cripple Creek for many years. Much of the rivalry was bitter, but in emergencies the rival cities stood together.

Victor's history was one of fortune and misfortune. Gold and glitter were mixed with tension and tragedy.

The first mines in the area to be later called Victor were discovered in 1891 and 1892.

By that time it was already known as the City of Mines because the largest and richest gold mines of the Cripple Creek Mining District were located on Battle Mountain just above Victor. Victor was platted in 1893. The new town was named Victor, after an early homesteader named Victor C. Adams. At first, there was no thought of creating a town but, as the population increased, it grew into a town. During those years, the entire area was covered by claims and prospect holes. Tents and shacks cluttered the landscape.

Finally, in 1893, the Woods Investment Company promoted the city. The area became organized in 1893 when the Woods Brothers purchased a 160-acre tract. Some say they were scoundrels. Others say they were pillars of the community. Either way, the Woods Brothers were promoters. The Woods brothers, Frank M. and Harry E., were mine owners and big spenders. It was they who did as much as anyone to develop Victor as a competitor to its sister, but larger city, Cripple Creek.

Within months, Victor was the second city in the district and closely rivaled Cripple Creek. The financial and political clout was in Cripple Creek and Cripple Creek attracted the newspaper reporters and writers. Victor was destined to live in the shadow of Cripple Creek.

The streets of Victor were paved with gold during the heyday of the 1890s gold rush. In the center of town, Frank and Harry Woods discovered the Gold Coin Mine while excavating for a hotel foundation and when the owners discovered they were excavating pay dirt they relocated the hotel and commenced mining.

Gold was found under the athletic field at Victor High School. In fact, some people dug gold out of their back yards. Rich ore was often turned up as basements for houses were dug. So much ore was nearby that the city fathers didn't bother mining the "low grade" stuff. It seemed as though gold was everywhere.

By 1896, Victor, with a population nearing 8,000, was well on its way to becoming one of Colorado's leading cities. Gold seekers jammed into town, paying as much as a dollar to sleep an eight-hour shift on a cot in a tent. The minute one man left another took his place. Saloons were open day and night and murder and suicide were so common in Victor that news of such atrocities ran as filler in the big city newspapers. Its hotels, churches, and homes were among the best in the region. Its citizens were proud of the new city hall, large jail, and abundant facilities.

Hotel Victor stood at the corner of Victor Avenue and Fourth Street. The lobby of Hotel Victor was a favorite meeting place during the 1890s when fortunes were being made and lost every day in the gold camp. It was always crowded. A fine city hall was constructed. There were many banks and churches. Saloons were everywhere and many were open twenty-four hours a day. The homes of many of Victor's residents were built high up on Battle Mountain close to the big mines.

Great mills to refine the gold ore were also built in the Victor area. They gave employment to many hundreds and made Victor an important milling center, too. During its boom days, Victor had several churches, Masons, Elks, Odd Fellows, and Unions.

Victor was a lusty gold camp. Its buildings were as elegant. Its saloons and whorehouses as wicked, its fires as disastrous.

Streetcars passed down Victor Avenue, the mining town's "main street" every few minutes. The main street had banks, shops, hotels, and the imposing Victor Grand, the District's largest and finest opera house.

Rodeo was a popular activity at Victor. Horse racing, too, was a favorite gold camp sport. It was the center of railroad and trolley cars. The area was unique among gold centers in that it was the only gold district in the world where a miner could go to and from the mines in trolley cars. During its peak years, nearly sixty trains and trolley cars passed through Victor daily. High line electric cars operated between Victor and Cripple Creek every hour from 6:10 a.m. until 2:10 a.m.

Among the many well-known people who have lived in Victor at one time or another, Lowell Thomas was the best known. Thomas grew up in Victor and graduated from Victor High School. Tobert Coates, art critic for the *New Yorker*, spent his early years in Victor. Winfield Scott Stratton, whose Independence mine made him the gold camp's first multi-millionaire, left his fortune to establish the unique Myron Stratton Home for the aged in Colorado Springs.

Victor became the second largest city in the district; only Cripple Creek was larger. False-fronted buildings stood shoulder to shoulder throughout the business district. There was much activity and growth was rapid. People clamored for a place to sleep. The boarding houses were packed. Miners stood in long lines at meal times.

Sadly enough, Victor's glorious history is marred by two of the most violent labor wars in history, which centered in Victor and the mines above the city. The Western Federation of Miners called the first strike in 1894 after several appeals to mine owners to correct the wage and hour inequalities at the mines. Some mines worked eight hours a day for their daily wage of three dollars. When the miners objected, The Pharmacist and other mines attempted to correct the situation in their own way, by lowering the wage of an eight-hour day to $2.50. The miners finally issued an ultimatum: Either establish an across-the-board basis of $3.00 for eight hours within ten days or a strike would be called. The mine owners ignored the ultimatum and the strike was called. There was some violence as a result.

The second strike called in 1903, was more violent and resulted in the downfall of the union. The mine owners immediately ordered a general close down of the mines, throwing nearly 4,000 miners out of work, The mine owners took full advantage of the situation, thus writing one of the saddest stories of Colorado history. Union men by the hundreds were rounded up and herded into "bull pens" little different from wartime concentration camps. Union leaders were beaten. A riot broke out in Victor with a few people being killed. Martial law was declared. Union leaders were deported to Kansas or New Mexico.

The mine owners won. The card system of employment was installed whereby a miner needed a card issued by the mine operators to gain employment anywhere in the area. No card, no job. The Cripple Creek area never recovered from the strikes.

Once again violence erupted on June 6, 1904. A bomb exploded in the depot killing thirteen people and injuring many others. The militia was called in. People were shipped out to the area by rail to Kansas and New Mexico with orders not to return. The labor war was over, but Victor never recovered. Mining officially ended in 1962.

## What It Is Like Today

Today's Victor is quiet, offering an authentic 1890s mining town getaway. Victor's modern-day treasures are the results of its rich gold rush history. Quite a few of its houses have been purchased by "flatlanders" for summer homes and there has been tourist traffic. As in the old days, Victor still lives somewhat in the shadows of its better known neighbor Cripple Creek.

## Remaining Buildings

The streets are lined with a wealth of history as 100-year-old buildings stand as legacy to the hustle and bustle of previous times. Some of its early buildings are well preserved. The Victor Lowell Thomas Museum houses artifacts and displays that depict the town's golden history, as well a room full of memorabilia from Lowell Thomas, America's celebrated radio and television journalist. Street-side benches and views from several historic interpretive trails offer a look at the golden era of the 1890s gold rush that made this area famous.

## How To Get There

6 miles southeast of Cripple Creek near Colorado Springs.

# Juicy Piece of History

On August 21, 1899, a fire broke out in Paradise Alley (in the Red Light District). Nearly four hours later, twelve blocks had been totally destroyed, including many of the buildings of the Gold Coin Mine. Estimates of the damage were huge. The rebuilding began immediately, this time with stone and brick. Twelve blocks of Victor's business district with some 200 buildings were totally demolished. Over 3,000 were left homeless.

A new Victor arose from the ashes. The business district was modern and progressive. The population had reached 7,000. The Red Light District reconstructed its brothels and cribs. The saloons were also rebuilt.

The next day dawned bright and clear in Victor. At the very first glint of light, hundreds of men went to work clearing away the ruins and building makeshift shacks. By noon, the new Victor post office was completed and people were getting their mail as usual. Almost before the ashes cooled, Victor started to build again. On the second day after the fire, more than 1,000 men were at work on a new Victor. Within eight months, a totally new city had been built. Victor then boasted a population of over 18,000. It became one of the most modern mining towns. It was also one of the nations' most prosperous places.

Section Two

# Ghost Towns
# of New Mexico

# 18

# Chloride

## History

An Englishman named Harry Pye, a mule skinner and prospector, was delivering freight for the U.S. Army in 1879, when he discovered silver in the canyon where Chloride is now located. He returned to the canyon with a few other prospectors and found the "Mother Lode," which was called the "Pye Lode." A tent city grew up nearby and then a town, originally called Pyetown, then Bromide. The name "Chloride" was finally selected, after the high-grade silver ore was found there. It became the center for all mining activity in the area, known as the Apache Mining District.

The area was occupied by Apaches, who were unhappy with prospectors and settlers invading their lands. Apaches attacked the Chloride store on January 18, 1881. Harry Pye would not live to enjoy his new found fortune. Just a few months after Pye found the mother lode, he was confronted by the Apaches, who attacked the store. When his pistol jammed as he tried to fend them off, he was killed.

More prospectors came to the area in January 1881, setting up camp at the mouth of Chloride Gulch. Soon, the men gathered, laid out an "official" town, and lots were distributed in a "lottery" by pulling tickets out of a hat. Chloride became the center of mining operations in the Apache Mining District, and by 1883, was called home to some 3,000 people. It had eight saloons, three general stores, restaurants, butcher shops, a candy store, a lawyer's office, a doctor, boarding houses, an assay office, a Justice of the Peace, a Chinese laundry, and a hotel. There was at least one brothel. The Pioneer Stage Line ran through town. *The Black Range* newspaper operated from 1883 until 1897.

Like other mining booms throughout the West, Chloride's life would be a short one. By 1893, the ore deposits were starting to play out and when the monetary standard was changed to gold, silver prices plummeted, mines shut down, and people left town. By the turn of the century, the city had only about 125 residents. The post office was open until 1956.

## What It Is Like Today

Though officially a "ghost town," the town is occupied by about twenty residents. Chloride also provides walking tours, a rest area, and RV Park for visitors.

# Remaining Buildings

Many buildings remain. Its historic main street is lined with false-front structures, as well as adobe buildings, some restored and some suffering the effects of time. There are two cemeteries in Chloride. The 200-year-old oak "Hangin' Tree" tree still stands. The Pioneer Store Museum still remains. The museum, situated in the original 1880 log building, features original store fixtures, pre-1900 merchandise, photographs, town documents, and numerous artifacts from early mining activities.

# How To Get There

To get to Chloride from Truth or Consequences, travel north on I-25 to Exit 83, then left on NM-181, left again on NM-52 and follow signs to Winston. Turn left in Winston at Chloride Road and travel southwest to Chloride.

## Juicy Piece of History

For the most part, the citizens of Chloride were quiet and peaceful. Chloride did, however, have a large tree called the "Hangin' Tree," which continues to stand in the middle of Wall Street. Perhaps it was this "threat" that helped to keep people in line. There is no record of anyone having been hung there. However, it was often utilized when rowdy or drunken cowboys or miners got out of hand. In those cases, the disorderly man would be dunked in the stock tank and chained to the tree until he came to his senses.

# 19

# Cimarron

## History

Cimarron was built upon what was originally the Beaubien-Miranda Land Grant. In 1842, Charles Lucien B. Maxwell, a fur trapper from Illinois, came to the area, working as a guide. His work often brought him to the Beaubien-Miranda Ranch, where he met and married one of Beaubien's six daughters, Luz in 1842, a shrewd move.

In 1864, after the death of his father-in-law, Lucien Maxwell bought out his five other heirs, and renamed the property the Maxwell Land Grant. He became the owner of the largest land grant in New Mexico. Consequently, Maxwell owned 1,714,765 acres and a house as large as a city block in Cimarron. His estate was three times as large as the state of Rhode Island. Buffalo Bill Cody was the goat ranch manager at one time for Maxwell.

When he first took over the grant Maxwell lost no time in getting a herd of cattle established. He industriously increased the herds by setting up individual ranchers with their own cattle; next, he set up tenants to make payments on a shared basis. It was typical of the times that no contracts were ever drawn up, all agreements being verbal.

He employed 500 men on the ranches, to work thousands of acres of rich land producing hay and other crops.

Money poured into his coffers, which was in truth a cowhide trunk in his bedroom, the rancher having little faith in banks.

The Maxwell House was built in 1864 and was soon the center of social life in Northern New Mexico as well as the principle "wayside inn." Clay Alison and Buffalo Bill occasionally came in from the lonely post on the goat ranch to live it up a little. It was in Cimarron that Buffalo Bill organized the first of his Wild West Shows.

Between the miners and the travelers along the mountain branch of the Santa Fe Trail, Cimarron quickly became a boom town, boasting sixteen saloons, four hotels and numerous trading stores.

Cimarron was officially established in 1861 and was named for the Spanish word meaning "wild" and "unbroken." The name was extremely fitting at the time, as Cimarron was quickly attracting mountain men, trappers, outlaws, gold seekers, traders, and cowboys. The city also gained a reputation for lawlessness with bullets flying freely.

Cimarron's post office was established in 1861. The Immaculate Conception Church was built in 1864 as a gift from Lucien and Luz Maxwell in memory of their deceased children.

Serving as cook for General Grant and President Abraham Lincoln during the Civil War, Henri Lambert drifted west in 1864 in hopes of finding gold. When the Land Grant Company discovered that Henri Lambert was operating a hotel and restaurant in nearby Elizabethtown, they asked him to come to Cimarron. Lambert moved to Cimarron in 1872 and built a hotel at a cost of $17,000. The Lambert Inn, as it was called at the time, started business in 1872.

Built during a time when law and order were non-existent, the hotel quickly gained a reputation as a place of violence, where it is said that twenty-six men were shot and killed within its adobe walls. Its saloon, restaurant, and forty-three rooms were witness to at least twenty-six murders during Cimarron's wilder days, most committed in "self-defense." Gangsters have all left their mark on the St. James, as attested by the numerous bullet holes in the ceiling of the main dining room.

The first question usually asked around Cimarron in the morning was: "Who was killed at Lambert's last night?" Another favorite expression following a killing was: "It appears Lambert had himself another man for breakfast."

A series of financial debacles started. Maxwell started the First National Bank of Santa Fe in 1870. It took him only a year to discover that banking was somewhat more complex than stuffing money into a cowhide trunk. He sold out at a heavy loss. Then, he was approached by a group seeking to finance the building of the Texas Pacific Railroad. Maxwell, the man born to raise hay and cattle invested $250,000. When it failed Maxwell retired to his ranch to lick his wounds.

Maxwell tried to cultivate the area but it backfired. In 1870, Lucien B. Maxwell sold his interest in the grant and all his properties for $700,000 and moved to Fort Sumner, New Mexico.

## What It Is Like Today

Schwenk's Hall, once a gambling house and saloon in the 1870s, is now a private residence and a gift shop. Within the residence is a plaque embedded in the wall that notes, "It was here that Coal Oil Jimmy (a stagecoach robber from Elizabethtown) and Davy Crockett won $14,000 bucking Faro."

In 1985, the St. James Hotel was restored and the old saloon, which is now used as the hotel's dining room, still holds the original antique bar, as well as twenty-two bullet holes in the pressed-tin ceiling. In the hall of the hotel is a plaque that commemorates Clay Allison and the roster of 19 men he was said to have killed. The hotel is open year around, with thirteen historic rooms, named for the famous and infamous people who once stayed there.

## Remaining Buildings

The museum, which was St. James Hotel, includes a variety of Indian artifacts, as well as items from the hotel. One of the most interesting historical sites is the Cimarron Cemetery. In the Lambert Family plot, surrounded by an old wrought-iron fence, rests Henri Lambert, who died in 1913. Lying next to him with a matching marker, is Mary Elizabeth Lambert, who died on December 8,

1926. Sitting in another plot away from Henri, is the crumbling white tombstone belonging to another Mary Lambert, Henri's first wife.

## How To Get There

Lies in Northern New Mexico off I-25, West on Highway 58. It is 55 miles east of Taos on Highway 64.

## Juicy Piece of History

Maxwell thought hard about building a colossal house. Noting the many prospectors, trappers, and travelers along the Santa Fe Trail who were camping just anywhere, he decided to build a huge stopping place for them. It was not a humanitarian gesture to shelter them from rain and snow. This was business. He would provide amusement for these lonely men, liquor to warm their bellies, male-female companionship, all with the intention of diverting the flow of gold to Santa Fe.

The Maxwell estate was three times as large as the State of Rhode Island.

# 20

# Colfax

## History

Named for Colfax County, this old settlement got its start in early 1908 when the New Mexico Sales Company, who were the developers for the St. Louis Rocky Mountain and Pacific Railroad, thought a profit could be made in developing the land. Heavily advertising the area as "on two railroads, near mountains, rich with game, and close to other towns," they thought the town would simply take off.

The site of Colfax was in the heart of rich farming land. It was situated on two railroads. Nearby mountains abounded in wild game for the hunter, and it was close to other towns. Despite all these resources, Colfax never really blossomed.

However, the promoters did have some initial success and by 1908, a post office was opened and soon, the small community had a school, church, a gas station, general merchandise store, and the Dickman Hotel (later known as the Colfax Hotel.) The town did stay alive for about twenty-five years from 1908 to 1933. The Great Depression of 1929 sealed its fate when gasoline prices forced people to give up driving. Most moved to one of nearby larger towns.

## What It Is Like Today

Colfax is abandoned and a few historic ruins can be seen.

## Remaining Buildings

Ruins of foundations, abandoned cars, and some shacks lie just off the highway.

## How To Get There

Located just 12 miles northeast of Cimarron and some six miles from Dawson, it is on Highway 64.

### Juicy Piece of History

Colfax never flourished as promoters had hoped. By 1921, the post office closed. Other businesses and people remained in the area until the Great Depression, when high gasoline prices forced most people to give up driving and the vast majority moved to the nearby towns that offered better advantages.

# 21

# Cuervo

## History

Cuervo began around 1901 when the CRI&P railroad came through Guadalupe County. The town began to grow as cattle ranching created a land boom. The population expanded as Route 66 came through. The highway created the additional trade of gas stations and hotels.

At its peak, Cuervo had two schools, two churches, two hotels and two doctors, along with numerous other businesses. In the 1930s, Cuervo had a population of almost 300. During the next decade, however, the population had already fallen to less than 150.

Things changed for Cuervo when I-40 came along. It buried much of the residential section of the town. Today, the area still supports around 50 people, who primarily live on the south side of I-40 and on outlying ranches.

## What It Is Like Today

Numerous buildings remain, mostly made of both adobe and stone.

## Remaining Buildings

The old school, church, and outbuildings remain. On the north side of I-40, where old Route 66 runs, there is an old abandoned gas station made from an old railroad car. The old combination post office/grocery store sits at the end of the road.

## How To Get There

Lies on Route 66

---

### Juicy Piece of History

Named after nearby Cuervo Hill, Cuervo is Spanish for "crow," which were abundant in the area.

# 22

# Dawson

## History

Coal was the resource that built the town of Dawson. By 1901, Dawson had a crew of fifty miners working on the first vein outcropping. There was also a saw mill, busy turning out lumber for houses. Dawson was well on its way to becoming a city and the center of the largest coal mining operation in New Mexico. A post office was established, with George Pearl being appointed as the first postmaster. There was a wine and liquor store and a town doctor. By 1902, Dawson's population was 600 with 40 children in the new school.

In 1903, a fire and explosion in a mine killed three miners. Still, the town grew.

The year 1905 brought a newspaper, the *Dawson News*. That year there was also enormous expansion of population and mine operations. There were now about 2,000 people living in the town and many new homes were constructed. The camp was largely populated by overseas immigrants: Greeks, Slavs, Italians, French, Welsh, Chinese, and more. Most of the single men, and those who had to make a stake before sending for their wives, lived in a separate section called Boarding House Row. There were segregated areas for different immigrants. Greeks and Italians were numerous enough to have their own divisions, presided over by a boarding boss of their own nationality, since many had not yet learned to speak English.

The Dawson Hotel got a seventy-foot addition. Coke, the solid portion remaining after coal is subjected to intense heat in a closed retort, was a major export to smelters and foundries all over the southwest.

About this time the Phelps Dodge Corporation began to show a strong interest in what was going on at Dawson. They bought it over. Under the new management the town expanded even more to a population of 3,500 and the "palatial" Dawson Theater was completed at a cost of $40,000.

There was plenty of work for everyone and Dawson seemed blessed above many other towns in the area. Yet, it was doomed to suffer a series of tragedies that shadowed its history to the end.

It was during this period of abundance and prosperity that Dawson suffered its worst catastrophe. In 1913 a tremendous explosion clogged the entrances and entombed 300 miners, killing 263. It happened at 3 p.m. There were no warnings, no escaping gas, only a sudden roar. Relief and disaster crews were rushed from neighboring towns and as faraway as Denver. By 11 a.m. the next day, 22 men were accounted for, with 16 being alive. As the days dragged on, the recovered dead outnumbered the living. Rescue workers worked round the clock, while rows of bodies brought to the surface grew longer. Distraught wives and family members clogged and impeded operations around the mouth of the mine. Two of the rescue workers were killed also. Mass funerals were conducted for the victims and rows upon rows of graves were dug, making it necessary to extend the cemetery far up the hill.

Even after such a calamity, life and coal mining went on in the camp and in time, some of the festivities resumed. The camp had always been a good show town and traveling theatrical companies found good audiences even shortly after the disaster.

Safety measures were heavily increased. Yet, in February 1923, another ruinous explosion took 125 lives. Again the cemetery had to be extended to allow more space for more rows of graves, the mass burials of 1913 repeated.

No further tragedy took place until the one of February 25, 1950. On that day the people of Dawson were told the Phelps Dodge Corporation would close down all operations. The announcement meant the death of the one industry town. The reason for the closure was simple—the increasing availability of a new fuel for smelters and foundries, natural gas. Many residents had already left and the town died.

## What It Is Like Today

Dawson has a few remaining buildings – life from its rich past.

# Juicy Piece of History

J.B. Dawson with his homestead, was one of the ranches with a few hundred acres each, who were giving trouble to the Maxwell Land Grant Company. He had bought a large tract from Lucien B. Maxwell. Land ownership was not documented. He found it 5 1/2 miles upstream from the settlement of Colfax and paid $3,700 to Lucien B. Maxwell for the deed, finalizing the verbal deal with a handshake. Having neglected to look into the matter of all the ranchers living on the land, Maxwell's party had no way of knowing who was a legal owner and who was merely squatting.

Matters began to gain heat when the company saw the ground was heavily laced with coal. The company wanted to develop the vein, but the attempted eviction of Dawson brought him up fighting, claiming he had bought his land from Maxwell although admitting the transaction had been purely verbal, sealed with a handshake. Maxwell he said, always did business that way and the company officials found he was right.

The matter went to courts. The case was tried in 1893 and the court decided in favor of Dawson. The New Mexico Supreme Court held that the company could not prove that Dawson did not own the land, or mineral rights thereof. Maxwell of course, could not testify as he had died eighteen years earlier.

Dawson set about marketing his coal in a big way. He began to sell the coal-bearing area to the newly organized Dawson Fuel Company for a township site. He held out 1,200 acres on which to build a home. By advice of counsel, Dawson had all transactions in black and white with all signatures duly witnessed. But his wife would not sign until she obtained full rights to sell all milk, for a period of ten years, the anticipated town of Dawson would need.

# 23

# Elizabethtown

## History

Ute Indians arrived at Fort Union in 1866. They wanted to trade "pretty rocks" for supplies. Captain William H. Moore was acquainted with one of the Indians. He had once found the Indian badly wounded and on the verge of death, given him water, and taken him back to the fort, where he was nursed back to health. This particular Indian was grateful to Captain Moore. He gave the Captain several of the "pretty rocks," which Moore quickly recognized as being rich in copper. The ore had been found on the upper slope of Baldy Mountain on the Western edge of the Maxwell Land Grant (see Cimarron).

"Where did you find these rocks?" asked Captain Moore from the Indian. The Indian agreed to lead Captain Moore to a spot high on the mountain, where enough copper was found to stake the first of many claims in the area.

While continuing to explore the area, three of the men made camp on the banks below. One of the men took a gold pan from his saddle bag and began sifting the creek gravel. There they were, sparkling gold flakes lying in the base of the pan. They wasted no time, immediately exploring the area, spending the next several days panning the creek and chipping at the rock. Since it was late fall, winter was about to come on the high slopes of the mountain. They vowed to keep their findings secret.

Alas! That was not to be.

They broke their pledge and word got out of the gold. When the snow melted in the spring of 1887 many other men were already flooding the area to find their fortunes.

Elizabeth town was the first incorporated town in New Mexico. The town was named after Captain William Moore's daughter, Elizabeth Catherine Moore, who had just turned four years of age but it was quickly nicknamed E-Town by most of the locals. Elizabeth Moore was the first school teacher and lived her entire life in Elizabethtown. By the end of July 1868, there were about 400 people living in Elizabethtown.

During the harsh winters, mining in the area was shut down and the town's population would rise and fall with the weather. Even when weather was good, the mining was erratic. When new gold was found, the town would grow as word spread and then fall again as interest dwindled. After the easy gold was picked, operations shut down.

The mines attracted many new residents including settlers from Texas who brought herds of cattle and made livestock raising another principal industry in the County. Soon there were 5 well-built stores, a drug store, 7 saloons, 3 dancehalls, 2 hotels, and a brewery.

The saloons had dance floors, gaming tables, and bars that were 100-200 feet long. A sawmill and several other stores followed, as well as saloons and gambling houses. Like most Old West towns, dancing, dining, and drinking were popular, as well as a burgeoning Red Light District. Women of "special virtue" worked their trade in second-floor rooms connected to the saloons.

By 1869, Elizabethtown had about 100 buildings. Enough families had joined the miners to require a schoolhouse and a Protestant church. A Catholic parish soon followed. By 1870, there were 7,000 residents.

Footraces and boxing matches were common events in the community.

The fever cooled as mining costs started to outweigh the volume of ore produced. Elizabethtown's post office was established in 1868, and was discontinued in 1931.

By 1875, Elizabethtown was a virtual ghost town but it was given a second chance in November 1878 when the Atchison, Topeka, and Santa Fe Railroad advanced its track into New Mexico. Now, ore could be shipped much cheaper. Investment in Elizabethtown area mines once again increased along with the population. The town was reborn.

One day, several well-mannered young men, riding good horses, flashing plenty of money, and claiming to be cowboys, arrived in Elizabethtown. The single women of E-Town were enraptured by their manners. These young men became part of the social life in several of the surrounding towns. Not until later, when they were captured, did townspeople learn that these young men were actually members of "Black Jack" Ketchum's outlaw gang. The notorious outlaw gang had terrorized the four-corner states in the late 1890s, robbing trains, stores, and killing men during their crimes or shoot-outs when they were threatened. Black Jack Ketchum was hanged in Clayton, New Mexico, on April 26, 1901, and is buried in the Clayton Cemetery.

By 1917, Elizabethtown's lifeblood was nearly drained. The mines no longer produced profits and the town folk had moved away, abandoning their homes, as no one wanted to buy them. Investors fell into bankruptcy and even the die-hard old timers left.

## What It Is Like Today

The eerie-looking beautiful remains of the once bustling boom camp look silently upon the Moreno Valley and the face of the imposing Baldy Mountain. There is a general store, several foundations and timber pilings from abandoned buildings. The Elizabethtown Cemetery is just about a mile up the road from the ruins.

## Remaining Buildings

The Elizabethtown Museum details Elizabethtown's brief but lively history, from the discovery of gold in 1866 through assorted gunfights to the town's slow fade after a dredge-mining project failed in 1903. The hotel ruins can also be seen.

## How To Get There

Elizabeth town is 4.8 miles north of Eagle Nest on NM 38.

# Juicy Piece of History

Here is an eerie story associated with Elizabethtown. Like many frontier towns of the West, Elizabethtown had its share of gruesome stories. Amazingly, it appears that the town housed a serial killer. Charles Kennedy, a big, husky full-bearded man, owned a traveler's rest on the road between Elizabethtown and Taos. When hotel guests came, they disappeared. After travelers registered at the rest stop, some vanished never to be heard from again. These traveling strangers were rarely missed in the highly transient settlement.

Evidently, when travelers stopped for a bed and a meal, Charles killed them, stole their valuables and either burned or buried their bodies. These events might never have been known, except for his wife's confession, when she fled from him in terror in the fall of 1870. The bleeding Ute Indian woman burst into John Pearson's saloon, where Clay Allison, Davy Crockett (a nephew of the American frontiersman) and others were whiling away the hours. Helping her to a chair, she told the story of how her husband had killed a traveler and their young son. Hysterical, she continued the shocking story telling of how her husband had been luring travelers, perhaps as many as fourteen, into their cabin and then murdering them.

On the day that she fled, she had witnessed another traveler who her husband had enticed inside by offering supper. During the meal, the passerby asked his hosts if there were many Indians around. Her unfortunate son made the fatal mistake of responding, "Can't you smell the one Papa put under the floor?" At this, Kennedy went into a fury, shot his guest and bashed his son's head against the fireplace. He then threw both bodies into the cellar, locked his wife in the house and got drunk. Terrified, the woman waited until her husband passed out, then climbed up through the chimney and escaped to tell her story. If his wife hadn't confessed, he might never have been caught.

Clay Allison, a local rancher, who was known for his gun-fighting skills, and almost always around when anything violent happened, led a group in search of Kennedy, while others were sent to search the house for evidence to support the woman's story. There were partially charred human bones still burning in the fire, and two skeletons beneath the house. Later, another skull was found nearby and a witness to one of the murders came forth. Kennedy, still drunk, was quickly found and taken into custody.

He was given a pre-trial. The court ordered that Kennedy be held for action by the grand jury, but rumors began circulating that Kennedy's lawyer was going to buy his freedom.

Three days later, Allison and his companions snatched Kennedy from the jail, threw a rope around his neck and dragged him by a horse up and down Main Street until long after he was dead. His body was not allowed by the townspeople to be buried in the Catholic cemetery and was interred outside the cemetery boundaries.

# 24

# Golden

## History

Golden was inhabited by Native Americans and Spaniards long before European settlers came to the area. Its real boom came in 1825 when gold was discovered. Golden was so named because it was the site of the first gold strike west of the Mississippi in 1825. Officially formed in 1879, Golden was selected as the center of the new gold-mining district.

In the late 1820s, two small mining camps developed as a result of the mineral finds. For several decades, though, nothing much happened in terms of investments. Eventually, large companies began to put money into the mines, bringing in numerous workers, followed by many individual prospectors.

The San Francisco Catholic Church was built around 1830. The town soon grew to support several saloons, businesses, a school, and even a stock exchange. In 1880, the post office was opened.

However, the expectations of Golden's miners were soon deflated, and by 1884, the gold was already beginning to dwindle and people began to leave the area. Even though the town began to experience somewhat of a decline, mining continued on a small scale until about 1892. The panic of 1893 spelled a doom for the town. Thereafter, ranching continued to be a mainstay of the economy.

By 1928, the population was so reduced that the post office closed. Golden officially became a ghost town. For years afterwards, many abandoned buildings remained, tumbling down between its few remaining occupied structures.

## What It Is Like Today

Today, Golden has seen a rebirth as new residents have moved into the area, building new homes and restoring others. Still, it remains a sleepy village with vivid reminders of its more robust past. Nearby Golden, are the traceable ruins of a pueblo called Paa-Ko that dates back to about 1300 A.D.

## Remaining Buildings

There are many original buildings and a great historic church. The Golden General Merchandise was opened in 1918.

# How To Get There

Golden is located along the Turquoise Trail Scenic Byway, about ten miles north of the Sandia Park junction on NM 14.

## Juicy Piece of History

Golden's most photographed building is the San Francisco Catholic Church, which was restored by historian and author Fray Angelico Chavez. He restored it while he was the padre of the St. Joseph Church in Los Cerrillos in the 1960s. Across the highway, west of the church are the ruins of the old stone schoolhouse.

# 25

# Madrid

## History

As many as 1,500 years ago the first Native American inhabitants mined the turquoise and lead deposits in the hills close to Madrid. Coal was found at Madrid as early as 1839. When General Stephen Watts Kearney came through New Mexico in the 1840s, he used Madrid coal for his army. By 1892, the yield was large enough to warrant the construction of a 6.5 mile spur from the Santa Fe Railroad.

In 1899, when the town had a population of 3,000, the Colorado Fuel and Iron Co. took control later selling to the Albuquerque and Cerrillos Coal Co., in 1906. At this time, the town housed 4,000 people. Providing the residents with most of all their needs, the company provided 160,000 gallons of water daily in tank cars. Railroad tanks brought water supply from springs five miles away. Sometimes the supply became exhausted and pipes were dry for a whole day until another tanker came in. Dishes, laundry and baths just had to wait. If you got too thirsty, the tavern was not too far away.

The company employed one doctor, who represented the entire medical facility for the town without hospitals or nurses. Every man paid a dollar a month for any medical care that he might need. When his wife had a baby he paid extra for the delivery.

In 1919, a man named Oscar Huber, who had worked for the company since 1910, was promoted as Superintendent of Mines for the Albuquerque and Cerrillos Coal Company in Madrid. He had a great deal of empathy for the miners. During Prohibition, the company even furnished a place where people could distill illegal liquor. Under his direction, Madrid residents enjoyed paved streets, a hospital, a company store, schools, and unlimited electricity from the company owned power plant in their homes. Under his capable leadership Madrid became a model for other mining towns to follow. He also formed the Employees' Club, athletic activities, and town events.

Coal production peaked in 1928. In 1936, when the owner was killed in a mine accident, Huber gained a controlling interest in the mine and continued to operate a friendly working environment for the employees. In 1947, Huber purchased the town of Madrid.

Madrid was deserted by the end of World War II, when natural gas became more widespread. By the early 1970s, Oscar Huber's son, Joe, by then, the owner of the entire town site, began to rent or sell a few of the old company houses to a number artists, craftsmen, and other individuals wanting to make their homes in the mountains. Determined to breathe new life into the town, he succeeded as more and more people moved into the area and Madrid was reborn.

## What It is Like Today

Over the decades, Madrid slowly revived. The arts scene has flourished and a real sense of community pervades the main street. This small village of about 400 residents is bustling during the summer months with shops, restaurants, and galleries catering to the many visitors along this ancient path.

## Remaining Buildings

Visit the Old Coal Mine Museum and wander among sinister looking machine parts and through dusty old workshops. A more vibrant remnant of Madrid's company town is the Mine Shaft Tavern where visitors can belly up to a forty-foot-long pine pole bar, over which hang murals by a local artist.

## How To Get There

Madrid is about 27 miles southwest of Santa Fe, New Mexico on NM 14. It is 13 miles beyond Golden.

# Juicy Piece of History

Electricity was unavailable for homes in Madrid in 1913. Generated in a powerhouse, the current was sufficient only for company houses. Families had to rely on kerosene lamps and candles. Cooking was done on coal fires, the fuel bought "reasonably" from the company.

Fire was always a hazard. Some houses burned through the use of lamps and candles. The company finally decided to wire them for electricity, but limiting them to a single bulb hanging naked from the ceiling, the "juice" turned on only at a given time after nightfall. In time, daytime electricity was allowed, for ironing, one day a week.

All this was before Oscar Huber. He changed everything and literally brought light to shine on Madrid. Huber had the main street paved and new houses built in all lots made vacant by fires. Then came a six-room hospital, first grade and high schools, to replace old residences used by students. Yet, no change in the gloomy, soot-blackened town was as spectacular as allowing all residents unlimited use of electricity.

In the first winter after this innovation Huber helped the people put on a Christmas display, the likes of which had never been seen in New Mexico. Huge figures were created of Mary, Joseph, and the infant Christ. Miners enthusiastically painted and wired them for electricity. As each Christmas came, new lights were added until in a few years, both sides of the canyon were covered with brilliantly lighted Biblical scenes.

The magnificent pageant drew thousands of visitors from other parts of the state, the show of lights maintained from early December through the New Year. The program set in motion by Oscar Huber gave the miners initiative to organize choral clubs with many fine voices and during evenings of Christmas week various groups were stationed at strategic points breaking into coordinated song with the words "let there be light." At that instant the main switch was thrown on and the dark old coal town broke into a blaze of glory and glad voices.

Madrid's Christmas lights were turned on for the last time in 1941. When the switch was thrown off at the end, the choraleers sang "Auld Lang Syne" while almost everyone wept openly.

Today, the Christmas lights tradition has been revived and attract people from nearby and faraway areas.

Madrid and the entire surrounding area are said to be haunted. Numerous ghost sightings have been reported. One often reported sighting is that of a silent cowboy who has often been seen escorting a Spanish woman, dressed in her best finery, down Main Street.

# 26

# Pinos Altos

## History

Prior to known discoveries of gold in 1836, Mexicans were said to have found rich deposits of the metal in a stream at the foot of an enormous cottonwood tree. They erected an enclosure for protection against Indians, the barricade constructed of materials at hand, which were adobe, stone, and logs. Men and animals were safely quartered inside at night while by day the men placered the gravels.

In July 1836, an old prospector named Adams staggered into the town of Pinos Altos. Bleeding from several gunshot and arrow wounds, the prospector rushed to a doctor. Lying on his death bed he told several friends who had gathered around him that he had been prospecting north of the town. His knapsack held a fortune in gold nuggets.

"I was prospecting for several weeks. There is a red hill and I saw gold lying everywhere," he explained. "I was filling up my knapsack with gold nuggets when an arrow struck the gravel at my feet. I hid behind some rocks. There were about a dozen Indians firing gunshots and arrows. I was wounded." He stayed hidden until nightfall and finally the Indians withdrew. Carefully making his way back to Pinos Altos, he traveled through streams to cover his trail.

Just a few hours after reaching Pinos Altos, Adams died from his wounds and was buried in the town's cemetery. When the gold in his knapsack was assayed, it was found to be worth over $7,000.

Word of the gold discovery quickly spread throughout the area and dozens of prospectors headed north in search of the red hill. However, no one ever reported finding the hill and its scattered gold.

Historian Dorothy Watson paints an idyllic picture of early day Pinos Altos. "They made of their homes a garden spot, there were fields of alfalfa, corn, and beans, and smaller plots of garden truck and flowers. Besides his terraced grapevines and fruit trees, Mr. Stanley had a rose garden. The Mexicans planted almond and peach trees around their homes and invariably had oleanders in tubs. During the summer they blossomed beside the doorways and somehow room was found for them in their small dwellings when frost came. They took fledgling mocking birds from nests, carefully tended and trained them. They were kept in large cages hanging outside on the walls where they called and exchanged confidences with the neighboring wild birds or complimented the guitar music. Each home had a small corral for a burro. Chickens and cows roamed at will, and here and there, goats would clamber over walls and roofs. Every day the yard was swept as clean as the mud packed earth floors of their dwellings."

The town never reached the status of being a "boom town" despite a population of 9,000 in the 1880s and 90s.

## What It Is Like Today

Pinos Altos began to show the usual signs of slowing down around the 1900s and today is only a memory of what was once a site of tall pines and running streams.

## Remaining Buildings

A few original buildings are there.

## How To Get There

Pinos Altos is located 6 miles north of Silver City on New Mexico Highway 15.

## Juicy Piece of History

When the Confederacy was established, the area including Pinos Altos was claimed by the South. There were many battles between the Whites and the Indians. As the town began to grow, Apache Indians beset it with frequent raids. It was during this period the settlers exhibited treachery of the worst sort. When a partially successful treaty had been established resulting in a certain amount of confidence on the part of the Indians, they were invited to attend a dinner to celebrate the signing of the treaty. Some sixty responded, entering the camp unarmed. As soon as all were seated, the host opened fire, killing many and maiming others.

One story in particular stands out. The Indian leader Mangas Colorado had been subjected to many indignities and treacheries by the settlers, blaming them as the reason for his continued attacks. General Carlton sent out word that Mangas Colorado must be captured "by any means deemed necessary." They located the Indian chief in the Pinos Mountains and conveyed the message to him that the new settlers were anxious to negotiate. The Chief went willingly. He was shot to death. With the chief out of the way, the soldiers found courage to capture his wife who was taken to Pinos Altos and killed.

From that time forward, the European settlers were in continued jeopardy until the establishment of military forts in the vicinity in 1869.

# 27

# Santa Rosa

## History

Santa Rosa, New Mexico, known as the "City of Natural Lakes," is called thus due to the many natural lakes and streams in the area. It developed mostly through ranch and agricultural farming.

The birth of Route 66 offered Santa Rosa a facelift. When Route 66 was completed through Santa Rosa in 1930, transportation services increased in the city. During the days of early Route 66, after travelers had tired of the long, hot, dusty miles, Santa Rosa became known as a welcome and well-known oasis in the desert. Travelers arrived in Santa Rosa to eat, rest, and perform car repairs, if necessary, at the many motels, cafes, and service stations that lined the highway. Various businesses began to come up as a way of serving transient travelers. The old road ran into town past the 81-foot-deep Blue Hole and Park Lake, a motorist campground and source of water during the Depression.

A second highway development took place in 1972. That year, I-40 opened through Santa Rosa. Though the city remained a busy off-ramp, many of the vintage Route 66 businesses began to die. A few continued to serve the exiting travelers off I-40. One of these was the Club Café that survived for almost another twenty years. Finally, the Club Cafe too, served its last meal in 1991. The Club Cafe stood vacant and soon fell into disrepair with the passing of time.

## What It Is Like Today

Recreational activities abound at the area lakes. Visitors enjoy all the amenities of a large man-made lake, such as boating, skiing, and camping at Santa Rosa Lake State Park. A side trip  is the ancient adobe village of Puerto de Luna, just ten miles south of Santa Rosa.

## Remaining Buildings

Today, there are plenty of signs reminding visitors of the past glory days of Route 66 that ran through Santa Rosa. While in Santa Rosa, a "must stop" is the Route 66 Auto Museum.

## How To Get There

17 miles from Cuervo.

# Juicy Piece of History

Santa Rosas's modern history can be traced to 1865. The town began as nothing more than a large Spanish Rancho, and was called Aqua Negro Chiquita. Sometime around 1890, it took a new name honoring a chapel built by Don Celso Baco. In 1940, when Steinbeck's epic novel, *Grapes of Wrath*, was made into a movie, director John Ford used Santa Rosa for the memorable train scene.

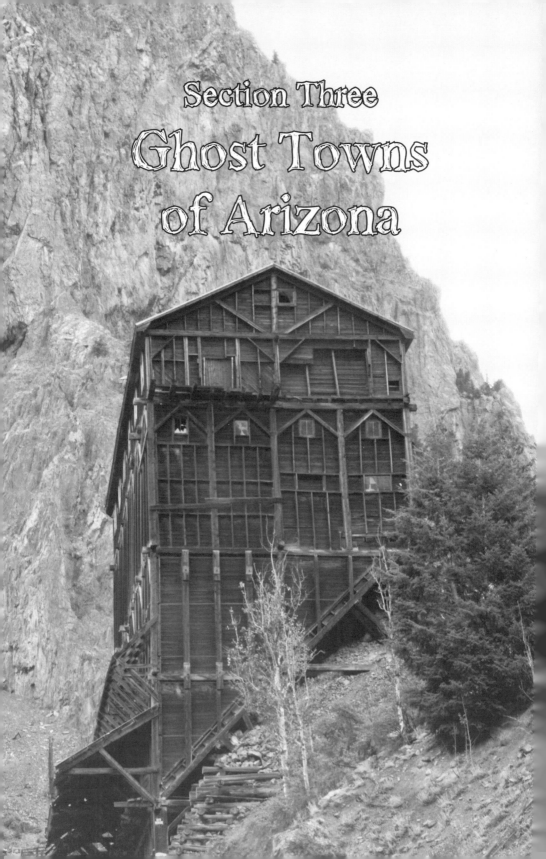

Section Three
# Ghost Towns
## of Arizona

# 28

# Chloride

## History

Chloride came to life in the early 1860s with the discovery of Chloride silver ore. The silver was found primarily at a site known as Silver Hill. But silver wasn't all that they eventually found. Gold, lead, zinc, and turquoise were abundant, too. It was the first mining camp of northwestern Arizona and one of the earliest in the entire state.

In 1871, Chloride became the Mohave County seat. Various types of businesses and transactions began to spring up in Chloride. In 1873, a post office was built. In 1898, the Sante Fe Railroad extended its tracks to Chloride, dramatically reducing the costs for ore and supply shipments. Just two years later, the town boasted a population of 2,000. These families were supported primarily by two major mines called the Tennessee and the Schuykill. Both these mines produced gold, silver, lead, and zinc on a major scale up into the late 1940s.

Just when a big silver boom had pumped the veins of Chloride full of blood, the deflation period set in. The demonetization of silver in 1893 affected Chloride, but didn't make it collapse. Chloride's peak years were between 1900 and 1920, when some 75 mines were in operation in the area. By the 1930s, the richest mine in the area was the Golconda, located between Kingman and Chloride.

The population escalated to approximately 5,000, but dropped to 2,000 around 1917. The town thrived into the 1940s but the closing of the Tennessee Mine signaled the end of large scale mining and prosperity of the town.

By 1944, the cost of materials and labor had increased to such a degree, that it became too expensive to extract the precious minerals from the surrounding area. The mines closed and the population declined dramatically. Within just a short period of time, Chloride was considered a ghost town.

The town did not die completely though. Chloride got revived in the 1960s. During the counterculture period of the 1960s a man named Roy Purcell painted what are now known as the "Chloride Murals."

## What It Is Like Today

This quaint "Old West" town is filled with gift shops offering handmade art, crafts, and jewelry. Many of the present day citizens are retirees, artists, musicians, and the like. There are still a few mines in operation today. The year-round population at Chloride is about 250, but peaks during the winter months at closer to 400.

## Remaining Buildings

The town prides itself on the preservation of buildings like the Jim Fritz Museum, the old jail, the historic post office, and the old train station. Chloride's Volunteer Fire Department, the oldest in Arizona, proudly displays its 1939 Ford Fire Engine to visitors. West of town is an old cemetery. There are ruins of the "House of Soiled Doves," which was the brothel from the old mining days.

## How To Get There

Chloride is 20 miles north of Kingman off U.S. 93 and 3 miles east of Grasshopper Junction on a paved road.

### Juicy Piece of History

In early times the prospectors were harassed by Hualapai Indians. In 1863 when the strikes were made the Hualapais killed four miners at Silver Hill camp by using guns for the first time. This situation with the Indians changed in the late 1860s. The U.S. Army took charge and began to subdue the Hualapai. Consequently, by the early 1870s a treaty was signed with the Indians, thus clearing the path for extensive mining.

# 29

# Fairbank

## History

In the 1700s, this area was the site of an Indian village called Santa Cruz. In the late 1870s, Fairbank was called Junction City when it began as a simple stagecoach stop. Later, it was called Kendall. In 1882, the town was renamed Fairbank for Chicago investor, Nathaniel K. Fairbank, who not only helped to finance the railroad, but also was one of the main organizers of the Central Mining Company in Tombstone. In 1882, it quickly became an important depot for the shipment of both cattle and the all important ore coming from nearby Tombstone. Fairbank served as an important railroad supply point and a stage terminal for mail and express. Most of its residents were working at the nearby Central Mining Company or the railroad.

In 1883, the post office was established in a building which also housed a general store and a saloon. Fairbank's importance as a railroad town grew. Before long, the community supported a Wells Fargo office, five saloons, four stores, three restaurants, a school, a jail, and a mill. The town also contained a steam quartz mill and a meat market. For those just passing through, the Montezuma Hotel was constructed in 1889.

Fairbanks lies on the Santa Cruz River. The river is subject to sudden flash floods. One of these floods occurred in September 1890 and the damage was all the more terrifying because it hit in the night when everybody was asleep. The *Tombstone Epitaph* reported the flood, the story recounting heroic efforts on the part of a Mr. Salcido, the owner of a lodging house. He was awakened by the roar of the waters and ran to each room, warning occupants to flee. "He had cleared the rooms and was leaving when the flood struck the front door and filled the house with water before he could get to the back exit to open the door and let the water run through. The water was up to his neck in a moment and he struggled until help arrived and saved him." The flood caused much property damage. However, the town rebuilt and continued to survive.

In 1900, the notorious Billy Stiles-Burt Alvord gang attempted a robbery in Fairbank. Their objective was to rob the Wells Fargo box from the express car of the train when it stopped at the Fairbank station to take on passengers. It backfired and the gang was forced to abandon the attempted robbery.

After the mining played out, Fairbank, like most of the other towns in the area began to die. The post office finally closed in the 1970s, but still the General Store remained opened for a number of years.

## What It Is Like Today

The old school house which has been restored, now serves as a museum. There are also a couple of old homes, a stable, and outhouses. A short hike will take the visitor to Fairbank's old cemetery atop a hill north of town.

## Remaining Buildings

The museum is a building from the past. The Grand Central Mill is still there. There are other buildings still remaining.

## How To Get There

Fairbank is located ten miles west of Tombstone on AZ 82, just east of the San Pedro River on the north side of the road.

## Juicy Piece of History

Fairbank had its share of lawlessness. One such incident was a train robbery that involved one of Arizona's most respectable lawmen, Jeff Davis Milton. In 1900, Milton was working for Wells Fargo as an Express Messenger. Many of the cargoes had gold and silver bullion. Part of Milton's job was to guard the laden rail cars.

Three bandits attempted to rob the express car while it stopped for water in Fairbank. In the shoot-out that ensued, Milton killed one of the bandits, wounded another, and stopped the gold from being stolen.

During the gunfight, Milton's left upper arm was shattered by a bullet. After the injury Milton was given the best attention locally, then hurried to a hospital in San Francisco where surgeons decided they would have to amputate the arm in order to save his life. Milton did not allow it. His arm was not amputated. Milton lived and regained partial use of it. He later joined the U.S. Immigration Service as a rider along the border.

# 30

# Harshaw

## History

David Tecumseh Harshaw was born in New York in 1828 and just 20 when he traveled overland to work in Nevada County mines. After the war, Harshaw traveled around looking for a good place to raise cattle, finally settling in Southern Arizona with about 1,000 head. He was grazing cattle in this area when he discovered a rich silver vein. In 1875, David Harshaw brought in a sack of dust and nuggets, the weight worth $843. It was a lucky find that gave him wealth overnight. It was the result of four days' labor for three men.

In 1877, people began to flock to the area. He called the mine "Hermosa." The Hermosa Mine was the lifeblood of Harshaw. His efforts proved profitable. Gradually, a mining community was formed, and Durasno was renamed Harshaw in honor of David Harshaw, who had become a prominent citizen.

Within six months the Hermosa Mill was crushing 75 tons of ore every day, making it the largest producer in Arizona. Six hundred people had arrived to share in the boom. Only 100 men listed themselves as miners. Twenty-four called themselves grocers, with the same number of liquor sellers. As for the females, only two kinds of work were given: housewives and prostitutes.

Lining the main and only street for three fourths of a mile were eight or ten stores, lodging houses, hotels, corrals, blacksmith shops, and thirty saloons. The town boomed with some 2,000 people.

A post office was established on April 29, 1880. There were also restaurants, laundries, stables, barber shops, and more. A town newspaper, the *Arizona Bullion*, furnished Harshaw residents with items of local news and other matters. The Harshaw population was youthful. Mike Fagan was the oldest man in town and was 45.

By 1880, David Harshaw had sold the claim and moved on. Having bequeathed his name on the one-time Mexican village of Durazno, Harshaw married Maria Jesus Andrada, the sister of his partner Jose. He died in 1884.

A series of cloudbursts which caused material damage, a major fire, and the closing down of the mine by the Hermosa Mining Company in 1881 contributed to a temporary slump in Harshaw's economy. The majority of the population moved on.

However, in 1887, Harshaw would see a minor rebirth when a man named James Finley purchased the mine for $600. Finley soon revived the mining, but on a smaller scale. The town then had about 100 people. A school, two stores, a meat market, three saloons, three boarding houses, and other buildings still operated. There were about twenty-five private houses. Finley worked the Hermosa Mine for a number of years. Then, the market value of silver declined in 1893, and Finley died in 1903. With his death, work stopped and the town died.

## What It Is Like Today

This is a ghost town, with nature claiming much of its remains.

## Remaining Buildings

Today, there are just a few remnants left of this old community, including the James Finley home, a tin-roofed adobe residence that is still occupied, a crumbling home, and the cemetery. There are mining remnants.

## How To Get There

Southwest of Patagonia, Arizona, all the way to the Mexican border.

## Juicy Piece of History

The Harshaw mining camp was built on a solid silver foundation. Indians living in the area called it "the enchanted land," because of streams flowing generously with clear water which provided an ample growth of good grass.

The padres who arrived next considered the area a fertile field for conversion. Then, the Spanish relinquished the country to the Republic of Mexico which put the padres out. The Mexicans left their adobe structures untended. Peach trees were lying here and there. When the Mexican families settled in the narrow canyon where the boom town of Harshaw would spring up, they found some of the trees and named their village Durazno for "place of the peaches." Later the area became a part of the United States.

# 31

# Jerome

## History

Like most places in Arizona, the area was first inhabited by Native Americans, as far back as 1100 A.D. Indians used the colorful Jerome azurite for facial decorations and pottery tinting over 1,000 years ago. Spaniards in the sixteenth century examined the minerals in the area and went on, since what they wanted was gold.

Later on, hostilities broke out between the Indians and the new settlers. By 1873, however, the Indians were defeated.

After the Mexican-American War ended in 1848 and the region became part of the United States, more and more Anglo-Americans began to settle the area. In came the ranchers, homesteaders, and more prospectors. In 1863, gold was discovered in the area and thousands of miners flooded the region. Jerome's modern era began in 1876.

Copper, the source of Jerome's wealth and prosperity, once boosted the fabulous metropolis to the fifth largest city in Arizona. A claim filed in 1876 really started the boom. It was leased to Governor Tritle of Arizona. Seeing that development was impossible without adequate backing, Tritle interested James A. MacDonald and Eugene Jerome of New York in forming a company.

Eugene Jerome was the grandfather of England's Sir Winston Churchill. Jerome had money and was willing to sink it in a rocky hole on Mingus Mountain but there was a string attached. He was positive a town would develop there and he thought it would be fitting and proper to have it named after him. In 1882, the United Verde Company was formed.

By 1899, the town was the fourth largest city in the Arizona Territory, featuring a hospital, schools, hotels, churches, saloons, and such refinements as electric lights, a railroad, a newspaper, and stylish Victorian homes for officials.

At this time, the town had 400 people and six saloons. For years, an almost continuous wagon train brought food, water, fuel, and mine supplies to the settlement that was progressing as it clung to an all but vertical mountainside. In 1900, a contract was let to supply Jerome with water on a regular basis with a 200-unit mule team.

The population was cosmopolitan to an extreme, represented by closely knit groups of Italians, Mexicans, Swedes, Yugoslavs, Bohemians, and Welshmen. No matter what group or location a man lived in, he had a magnificent view of Verde Valley with its red backdrop of Oak Creek Canyon. Only one main street existed, wrapping itself around the crest of the ridge and most cross streets were steep stairways.

When the value of copper took a tumble in 1884, the mine closed. It was a short-lived slump, however. The mine was bought over and started producing again. Montana's Senator William A. Clark was attracted by the United Verde, soon bought the mine, and began the intensive mining operations that quickly reaped fame and fortune for Jerome.

Apparently, the devaluing of copper did not affect the growth rate of Jerome, since the first school was started that year. Some people left, but, the town hung on and continued to grow slowly. By September, 1883, a post office was established, which has never closed.

When the town was incorporated, one of the laws to be pushed forward related to building codes, in order to prevent fires. Requiring brick or masonry construction, the laws of 1899 were instituted to end the frequent fires that plagued Jerome previously. Jerome never had gas. It jumped directly from kerosene to electricity.

When World War I began, the price of copper soared and it was then that the town really boomed. More copper was coming out of Arizona than any other state. As copper demands increased Jerome flourished. By 1929, the population soared to 15,000 and included a working force of 2,345 men. Jerome's peak population of 15,000 was reached just prior to the depression years. By this time, Jerome had four grocery stores, six dry goods stores, six lodging houses, seventeen saloons, a telephone company, and all types of professional men, with skills from photography to dentistry. Along with the saloons and brothels there were also three movie theaters, schools, swimming pools, bowling alleys, restaurants, churches, and an opera house.

Jerome was a mix of the rowdy and culture. Considering the rough type of characters attracted to mining communities and the amount of liquor usually consumed, Jerome maintained fairly good law and order. A scuffle occurred once between Jack Habercorn, known as "Happy Jack" and Bob Williams. It resulted in Jack stabbing his adversary with a candlestick. It resulted in minor injury but a trial was held in one of the saloons. The Justice of the Peace was Major Oatie. Since it was the judge's first trial held in Jerome, he felt a certain amount of leniency was in order. "Happy Jack" was fined the drinks for the house.

Jerome suffered from labor troubles. The first strike was in 1907, a success for the men which reduced the ten-hour work day to eight and raised wages to $2.75 a day. There was another strike in 1927. The men not only ceased to work, but staged demonstrations and street battles.

After the war, the price of copper ore began to decline and had become harder and harder to extract from the mountain. By the time the Great Depression began, Jerome, along with the rest of the nation was in a full-blown depression and by 1930, the mines had closed. As the price of copper went hurtling downward, the main mine closed in 1932 and work ceased.

There was a price for prosperity. Smoke from the smelter was so acrid that all vegetation died on Cleopatra Hill, including oak and pine trees. People gagged on the toxic sulfurous fumes. Buildings collapsed due to the constant blasting.

World War II, copper prices increased once again, putting the town "back in business." But, the rich copper ore was dwindling and getting even harder to get to. After the war, prices dropped once again. In 1953, Phelps Dodge permanently closed the big mine and that was the end of Jerome as a city. Only 100 remained of the 15,000. Jerome seemed doomed.

With no work, families moved away in the masses. Many, with no buyers for their homes, simply left them, complete with furnishings, before making their way on to other opportunities. Buildings began to deteriorate, continued to slip down the hill, or suffered vandalism over the next two decades.

The physical "shifting" of the town has been gradual since a mighty dynamite blast was set off underground in 1925. Since then Jerome's famous Traveling Jail has slid about three hundred feet and some houses have moved at the rate of four inches per year.

It might have been the end had not a group of enterprising citizens organized the Jerome Historical Society and proclaimed Jerome to be America's newest and largest ghost city.

Today, Jerome attracts thousands of visitors annually. Perhaps Jerome's uniqueness is due to the fact that ever since the dynamite blast in 1925, the town has been gradually slipping downhill. Some buildings, having moved many feet from their original locations, contribute greatly to Jerome's attraction for tourists.

# What It Is Like Today

Jerome has survived by becoming a mecca for artists and tourists. Today, this quaint town of about 400 residents provides tourists with not only a view of the past in its numerous historic buildings, but also a number of specialty shops, restaurants, and galleries. One interesting area is the "Crib District" across the street from the English Kitchen, in a back alley where all the buildings were part of Jerome's Red Light District.

# Remaining Buildings

Jerome provides a number of attractions including the Douglas Mansion State Park and a 1916 mansion and museum. The cemetery offers a beautiful view over Jerome. The stones and markers give testimony to the universality of the lure of mineral wealth: natives of Italy, Germany, Russia, and Ireland are buried there.

# How To Get There

Jerome is located between Prescott and Flagstaff on AZ Alternate 89. Jerome is 33 miles northeast of Prescott on U.S. 89A.

# Juicy Piece of History

With World War I, the need for copper soared. From all over the world, immigrants came to the copper mines that were operating 24 hours a day in Jerome. A number of hotels were built for the sole purpose of housing the miners. Many of the town's businesses also operated around the clock, especially the "shady" ones. The shady businesses included 8 brothels, 21 saloons, and numerous opium dens. Jerome earned a wicked reputation. In fact, the chaos increased with even more prostitution, alcohol, gambling, drug abuse, and gunfights in the streets as the population continued to grow.

Filled with wooden buildings, two blocks of the commercial district burned in 1894 and more fires blazed businesses in 1897, 1898, and 1899. One interesting tale of the 1897 fire was when a madam of one of the local brothels ran into the street in a panic, offering free "business" to the entire fire department from then on if they would save her house. Not surprisingly, the house was saved.

Jerome quickly gained a reputation of a rough and rowdy town, with its many saloons, gambling dens, and brothels, so much so that on February 5, 1903, the *New York Sun* proclaimed Jerome to be "the wickedest town in the West."

# 32

# Kingman

## History

Lewis Kingman was a railroad surveyor. When the railroad began to reach Arizona, Lewis Kingman surveyed the route between Albuquerque, New Mexico, and Needles, California, in 1880. In 1882, a settlement cropped up along the railroad tracks. The fledgling town was named after Lewis Kingman. Once the railroad tracks were complete, more new businesses began to pop up, including a hotel, several tent buildings housing a restaurant, a saloon, and a mining operations office. Soon, a post office was also established.

In 1886, Kingman built its first school. The next year the town's first church was born and the opening of the Kingman Hotel took place. In 1887, Kingman won the election of county seat for Mohave County. By the turn of the century, Kingman had grown to some 500 people and continued to develop as gold was discovered in the hills surrounding the town. By the end of World War I, mining had dropped off and Kingman began to suffer.

## What It Is Like Today

Today, the Kingman area is home to some 40,000 people with numerous recreational opportunities nearby.

## Remaining Buildings

A visit to the old powerhouse, which has been converted to a Route 66 Museum and visitor's center is worthwhile. The Powerhouse Building is also home to Arizona's Route 66 Association. The historic Hotel Brunswick, which was originally built in 1909, has been serving customers for almost a century. Another interesting building is the White Rock Auto Court, one of the last auto court motels on Route 66.

## How To Get There

Lies on Route 66.

## Juicy Piece of History

The Beale was the leading hotel in Kingman. It first catered to the many passengers of the railroad and later to travelers of Route 66, when it came through. Successful for decades, the historic Hotel Beale now sits lonely and abandoned.

# 33

# Oatman

## History

Gold was first discovered in Oatman in 1902 by a man named Ben Taddock. Taddock was riding along the trail, when he saw free gold glittering on the ground. Losing no time, he immediately filed a claim. A tent city soon sprang up as other miners heard of the gold find and flocked to the area. In its earlier days, Oatman boasted a narrow gauge railway.

Taddock, however, lacked the funds to develop a mine, so he sold his claim in 1903 to Judge E.M. Ross and Colonel Thomas Eqing, who in turn sold it to the Vivian Mining Company.

The Drulin Hotel was built in 1902, and served the area miners. This old hotel, now called the Oatman Hotel, is still in operation today. With the discovery of the Tom Reed gold mine in 1908, the town became known as Oatman. There were about 150 people at the time. The post office was changed from Vivian to Oatman in 1909.

A story is told of the courageous tenacity of a miner who lost his eyesight. Henry Ewing continued to work his Nixon Mine, located near Vivian, despite his handicap and the warnings of concerned friends. He set up guide wires to assure himself a degree of safety, and then proceeded to sink a shaft. Completely unaided, Ewing drilled, blasted, mucked, hauled ore buckets to the surface, and cared for himself at his camp. He experienced two narrow escapes with death, once when he unexpectedly encountered a rattlesnake and another time when he fell thirty feet from a ladder.

In its heyday, Oatman was one of the largest producers of gold in Arizona. The town had its own paper, the *Oatman Miner*, as well as dozens of other businesses.

In 1921, a fire burned much of Oatman, but the town was rebuilt. Just three years later the main mining company, United Eastern Mines, shut down operations forever. But with the birth of Route 66, Oatman hung on, catering to the many travelers along the new highway. By 1930, it had two banks, seven hotels, twenty saloons, and ten stores. There were nearly 20,000 people living in Oatman area.

## What It Is Like Today

Oatman today is a tourist town. The main street is lined with shops and restaurants. Gunfighters perform daily, displaying blazing six-gun shootouts in the middle of main street. There are about 100 people living in Oatman year round now.

## Remaining Buildings

There are a few remaining buildings from its colorful past. Some have been restored while others are being claimed by mother nature.

## How To Get There

When traveling westbound Route 66, Oatman Highway continues another 20 miles to Golden Shores.

## Juicy Piece of History

Oatman was named for a family which had camped near Gila Bend in 1851. Royse Oatman, his wife, and seven children were attacked by Apaches while they were on their way to California that year. The father, mother, and four of the children were murdered. Twelve-year-old Lorenzo was thrown down a small cliff and left for dead, and sisters Olive and MaryAnn were captured and sold to the Mohave Indians as slaves.

When a detail of soldiers were sent out to effect their rescue, the sisters, Olive and Mary Ann were hidden by their captors at a small spring a half mile north of town and then spirited away. Mary Ann died in captivity but apparently Olive adapted to her surroundings and even married a Mohave. There is a photograph of her with marriage tattoos. She was twenty when her brother found her. She had Indian tattoo marks on her chin when the brother found her. Olive was rescued in 1857 near the site of the town.

Lorenzo, who survived the massacre, organized a group to secure Olive's release from the Mohaves. Some say that she was not "rescued" at all. Olive knew that a party had been out looking for her for some time, and she eventually walked away from her "captors" to rejoin her brother. Olive was released in 1856 and joined her brother at Fort Yuma.

There are two versions to Olive's life story after that: One has her eventually marrying an Anglo in 1865 and dying in Texas in 1903. The other story claims she went insane after being forced to leave her Indian family and died in an asylum only a few years after her rescue.

# 34

# Pearce

## History

The Commonwealth Mine was the mainstay of Pearce, discovered by Cornishman Jimmie Pearce. A town grew up near Jimmie Pearce's Commonwealth Mine. A post office opened on March 6, 1896. Soon, the population rose up to 1,500. Peak production of the Commonwealth was realized quickly in 1896, but it would continue to operate for years after that. Other businesses included a school, hotels, and several saloons. Pearce even had its own motion picture theater. Jimmie Pearce sold the Commonwealth for $250,000.

The Great Depression took its toll and in the early 1930s; the mine closed and the railroad pulled up its tracks. Pearce was the last of the Arizona gold rush camps.

## What It Is Like Today

The area is seeing rejuvenation as retirees and others are attracted to the climate and are buying real estate here. The old post office, decommissioned in the late 1960s is now a private residence. The historic general store is now re-opened.

## Remaining Buildings

Remaining buildings include the post office, school, jail, some foundation and the Old Store built in 1894 by Soto Brothers & Renaud. Pearce Cemetery is west of the town along Middlemarch Road.

## How To Get There

Pearce is 9 miles north of Courtland and 29 miles northeast of Tombstone. Coming from the other direction, it is 22 miles south of 1-10 on US 666, exit 331.

# Juicy Piece of History

Pearce is named after Jimmie Pearce who was a miner in Tombstone. Together with his wife who ran a boardinghouse, he had saved some money to buy land, and he bayed a ranch lot northeast of Tombstone.

After carefully saving their money, they purchased some ranch land in the Sulphur Springs Valley northeast of Tombstone and settled down to the ranching life along with their three children.

One day in 1894, Pearce found placer gold beside a hilltop and he was back in the mining business, not as a worker but as owner. He wasn't even looking for gold. He called his new mine the Commonwealth and when word spread of his find, the area flooded with new residents.

Jimmie Pearce, however, didn't stay in the business long. He sold the Commonwealth Mine for $250,000 to a man named John Brockman. His wife, however, remembering some of the hard times they had lived through in the past, insisted on a clause in the contract that guaranteed her the right to run a boardinghouse beside the mine.

Section Four

# Ghost Towns of Wyoming

# 35

# Bonneville

## History

In May of 1832, Captain Banjamin Bonneville left Fort Osage, Missouri, with an expedition consisting of 110 men and 20 wagons headed for the Rocky Mountain West. Upon his arrival in the Green River Valley he ordered immediate construction of a fort along the west bank of the river.

Bonneville was dubbed "Fort Nonsense" and "Bonneville's Folly." Many thought that it was a poor location for a fort. It was soon abandoned due to the severity of long Wyoming winters. However, the fort commanded a strategic location in the heart of the Rocky Mountain Trapping System. Completed in September 1832, Fort Bonneville was one of the first permanent structures built by the new settlers in Wyoming. In 1833, it was the center of trading activity for the annual rendezvous. In 1836, it became the storage for the rendezvous.

## What It Is Like Today

Bonneville lies off the highway and is a semi ghost town. There is a modern plant that is operational where some work is being done. The houses are abandoned and the rail tracks are still visible. A handful of houses are occupied.

## Remaining Buildings

The remaining buildings seem more like they are from modern times, mostly houses built in the 1900s.

## How To Get There

Bonneville is in Fremont County, north of the Shoshone, in the Riverton metro area. Bonneville and Shoshoni are neighbors.

## Juicy Piece of History

Bonneville appears to be one those towns that lie in the middle of nowhere in Wyoming. Nevertheless, it is a beautiful town with a few remaining buildings showing signs of life.

# 36

# Cheyenne

## History

Cheyenne is Wyoming's oldest city and also the largest. When the Union Pacific Railroad came through on its way to the West Coast, General Grenville M. Dodge and his survey crew platted the site. By the time the first track was built into Cheyenne four months later, over 4,000 people had migrated into the new city. Most of the construction gangs were ex-Civil War soldiers who had come from the distant East. They couldn't get home and back in that period of time. Therefore, they poured into Cheyenne for the winter, swelling its population to over 10,000, virtually overnight.

Because Cheyenne sprang up like magic, newspaper editors visiting from the East called it the "Magic City of the Plains." Cheyenne was declared the territorial capital in 1869. The next year Cheyenne began loading cattle onto trains for shipment east, and within a few years, the city was the hub of Wyoming's ranching industry. The name likely came from French trappers in the region many decades earlier who did not like a particular Native American tribe and intentionally gave them the French name "chienne," which meant wild dog in a derogatory way.

Cheyenne was a major national source for beef during the 1870s and 1880s. The cattle industry boomed when European and East Coast investors bought up all the land around Cheyenne for grazing. By 1885, the city bathed in its wealth and was known officially as "Wall Street of the West." Anything that happened with the cattle industry directly affected New York's Wall Street and the eastern states' economy.

Francis E. Warren was a successful businessman in Cheyenne. He became Wyoming's Senator for thirty-seven years. Upon his death, the name of the fort, which was earlier called Camp Cheyenne, was changed to Francis E. Warren on January 1, 1930. It is currently one of the nation's strategic missile installations, aiding in Cheyenne's economy.

In 1886, the Union Pacific was pushed into building the most beautiful railroad depot between Omaha and San Francisco. It became a National Landmark in 2006. The portico in the inside of the building was a popular European feature. It was designed to allow horse-drawn carriages to go into the building to let out passengers without fear of them getting rained or snowed upon. The building is now the Cheyenne Depot Museum.

The gold rush of 1877 further promoted Cheyenne's growth as a stop for stagecoach and freight traffic. Buffalo Bill Cody used Cheyenne as a staging place for his Wild West show. In a celebration of the cowboy, Cheyenne Frontier Days was begun in 1897 and, with its success, has become the world's largest outdoor rodeo.

Saint Mary's Catholic Church was built in 1909. Saint Mark's Episcopal Church was built in 1888 with Gothic revival elements, pointed arch windows, and stained glass windows. St. Mark's was the religious, cultural, and social center of early Cheyenne.

The boom turned to bust during the severe winter of 1886-87, when nearly eighty percent of the estimated one million head of cattle in the area perished because of a severe winter. The Cattle Barons went broke.

From the 1920s through the 1950s, Cheyenne's expanded rail yards and facilities employed as many as 5,000 men and women in around the clock shifts.

# What It Is Like Today

Cheyenne is very much alive and functioning today. Today, the cattle and sheep industry around Cheyenne is very strong, adding to the economy. From humble beginnings, it has become a Wild West celebration during the last ten days of July every year. Contests of steer roping and bronco riding still prevail, along with Brama Bull riding and Wild Horse races. Cheyenne rail yard is still a major hub for the Union Pacific as over sixty-five coast-to-coast trains pass through it daily.

# Remaining Buildings

The city has four National Register Historic Districts encompassing approximately 1,200 structures. Cheyenne preserves one of the last surviving Union Pacific Big Boy locomotives ("4004"), some of the largest steam locomotives ever built, designed for hauling freight over the Rocky Mountains at high speeds. The locomotive now resides in Holliday Park in central Cheyenne. Historic homes include elaborate mansions built by wealthy cattle barons from the East and abroad during the late nineteenth century.

Some of the other remaining buildings include:

Atlas Theatre was built in 1887. This three-story building originally held a confectionary shop on the lower level and the upper floors were utilized as office space. In 1907, it was converted into a theatre. It is placed on the National Register of Historic Places. The Atlas Theatre building is located at 211 W. 16th Street.

St. Mark's Episcopal Church is Cheyenne's Episcopal congregation. It first held services in a small frame church in 1868. However, by 1886, the congregation, made up of a number of cattle barons and large ranchers, had begun to outgrow the small building and plans were made to construct a new one. The new one was opened in 1888. The church is located at 1908 Central Avenue.

The Nagle-Warren Mansion, located at East 17th Street, is one of Cheyenne's most elegant residences, was built in 1888 as the home of Wyoming businessman, governor, and senator, Francis Warren.

# How To Get There

Cheyenne is 47 miles North of Fort Collins, CO, on I-25.

# Juicy Piece of History

The Wyoming Telephone and Telegraph Company published the first telephone directory in the United States in Cheyenne in 1881. Due to a shortage of white paper, it was printed on yellow paper instead, which started the tradition of the "yellow pages" phone directory.

A luxurious hotel opened in 1911 called the Plains Hotel. When a newly married couple checked in here years ago, the bride caught her groom with another woman, and after killing them both, she turned the gun upon herself. All three are said to haunt this historic hotel.

Alferd Packer, the only American ever convicted of cannibalism (though the official charge was murder since cannibalism is not a crime in the United States), was apprehended north of Fort Laramie and was taken to jail in Cheyenne, March 11, 1883.

Cheyenne's Nellie Tayloe Ross, in 1924, became the country's first woman Governor.

There is an interesting story behind the construction of the bell of St. Mark's Episcopal Church in Cheyenne. In 1924, two Swedish men were hired to complete the tower. However, when it was forty feet high, the two masons simply disappeared.

When new workers were hired they immediately began to complain of hearing strange tappings, the sounds of hammering, and whispers coming from the very walls of the tower.

Years later, a man came forward explaining that when the original masons were working on the tower, one of them slipped and fell to his death. The other, panicked that he would be deported, entombed the man's remains in the tower wall.

A psychic who visited during this time reported sensing two spirits in the tower, one of whom was very upset, and the other, an elderly white-haired man who walked with a cane. The two spirits are thought to be the mason that fell to his death, and Father Rafter, who had hired the men.

# 37

# Cody

## History

Early day land developers in northern Wyoming saw Buffalo Bill as probably the most advertised man in the world and invited him to head their venture in developing modern-day Cody. William Cody, better known as Buffalo Bill, responded, for he saw the potential of tourism and recreation possibilities in the area. He poured large amounts of his own money into the town of Cody and built a magnificent hotel, named the Irma Hotel after his youngest daughter. The hotel cost Cody a staggering $80,000, which in 1902 was a large amount of money. The famous Irma Hotel accommodated well-heeled big game hunters, Yellowstone Park sightseers, and the affluent ranchers who came to town. Cody had the enormous cherrywood back bar imported from France, shipped by rail to Red Lodge, Montana, and brought by wagon to Cody. Cody also built a hunting lodge, which he called Pahaska. That, too, is still in existence.

In 1902, the railroad was built to Cody and a wagon road from Cody to Yellowstone was under construction.

To bolster the economy of the struggling new town, Colonel Cody persuaded his friend, President Teddy Roosevelt, to establish the Bureau of Reclamation and to build the Shoshone Dam and Reservoir, later renamed the Buffalo Bill Dam and Reservoir. With the completion of this dam, the highest in the world at the time, the community was established soundly in the irrigation and electric power fields. Also through his friendship with the President, Buffalo Bill helped establish the first National Forest, the Shoshone, and the first Ranger Station, at Wapiti. The organization in 1901 of the Cody Club, Cody's Chamber of Commerce, the Cody Stampede and Rodeo in 1922, the dedication of the various structures of the Buffalo Bill Memorial Association, including the Gertrude Whitney Statue of Colonel Cody in 1924, the Buffalo Bill Museum in 1927, and the Whitney Gallery of Western Art in 1959, have all been steps in the development of the city.

## What It Is Like Today

The town of Cody is very much alive, and a fascinating place to visit. There are about eight thousands residents living here year round. There is a daily Rodeo during the summer months. Plenty of gift shops decorate the town. There are also campgrounds, schools, banks, and all other businesses of a modern, functioning town.

Hotel Irma was built for Buffalo Bill's daughter. During summer months there is a gunfight show in front of the hotel for visitors to see.

Buffalo Bill Museum, Cody, Wyoming.

## Remaining Buildings

The Buffalo Bill Museum contains 5,000 items in its biographical and Western collections. About 1,500 firearms are displayed at the Cody Forearms Museum, a study collection that shows the technology and aesthetics of firearms, with representatives from the entire history of projectile arms from crossbows to modern automatic weapons.

## How To Get There

Just fifty-two miles east of Yellowstone Park, Cody, Wyoming, can be found in the northwest quarter of Wyoming.

### Juicy Piece of History

William Cody (1846-1917) was born in 1846. As a frontiersman, whose career included riding for the Pony Express at the age of 14, he acquired his nickname while hunting bison to feed railroad crews. He worked as a scout for the army and helped fight Indians in Colorado and Wyoming. Colonel William F. "Buffalo Bill" Cody first entered the Big Horn Basin of Wyoming in the 1870s. The Colonel and several friends came to the area with the purpose of land development and the building of a community. The site was named Cody in 1895.

William F. Cody received the appellation "Buffalo Bill" as a result of serving as a buffalo hunter for the Kansas-Pacific Railroad.

When Cody was only 11, he killed his first Indian. Buffalo hunters were employed to provide meat to the railroad workers and soon Cody became a buffalo hunter. During the seventeen months he was with the railroad, he killed 4,280 bison.

Thus, Cody was an experienced rider at age 15 when he answered an advertisement seeking riders for the newly created Pony Express. Cody was assigned to Slade's Division. The Division the longest leg on the route, extending from Red Buttes Station to Rocky Ridge Station. When Cody's relief rider was killed, Cody covered a distance of 322 miles in 21 hours, 40 minutes using 21 horses.

# 38

# Encampment

## History

Encampment (Grand Encampment) was originally a trapper's rendezvous. As early as 1834, some trappers regularly worked the streams on both the Atlantic and Pacific drainages of the Sierra Madres, gathering pelts for the Rocky Mountain and America Fur Companies. They held a rendezvous at the upper end of the North Platte Valley and called the area at the foot of the Sierra Madres Camp le Grand, which later became Grand Encampment.

After the mountain fur trade dwindled to a close in the early 1840s, the Grand Encampment Valley saw little use. Colorado Utes ranged into the area and one branch of the Cherokee Trail brought travelers through on their way to California during the 1849 gold rush.

The first permanent White settlers moved into the Grand Encampment Valley in the 1870s. The mining boom at Grand Encampment started in 1879, when sheep lender Ed Haggarty found copper several miles west of town on the west side of the Continental Divide. Hordes of miners and speculators flocked to the area, raising a town called grand Encampment. Hundreds of mine shafts went down into the rocky soil.

In 1900, the Godsell Custom smelter was erected. Although the town was located on the river, the smelter was built about five miles from the main fork. This necessitated constructing a wooden pipeline to solve the water problem of the plant. Through this flume system, it was claimed that 1700 horsepower was developed, which in turn generated 1200 horsepower of electrical energy. The town boasted it had the cheapest electricity per capita of any city in the U.S.

The town was the center of culture and business. There were literary clubs, a school, dance halls, thirteen saloons, market places, and offices. The mining companies, some thirty-one of them, transacted their business here. The *Encampment Herald* claimed the consumption of lumber in 1902 to 5.5 million feet. At this rate, things ran pretty lively until 1908. The Saratoga and Encampment Valley Railroad engines came whistling in for the first time that summer. Willis George Merson promoted the idea of selling mine shares by the thousands. In 1903, the Ferris Haggarty had sold for a half million dollars, but by 1908, from 20- to 30-million worth of stock in this mine had been issued. The company was hauled into court that same year for over capitalization and fraud.

Speculation, dishonesty, and cupidity have brewed. That fall most other mines had closed their doors. Litigation, long and costly, started in 1909. Soon, Encampment's population dwindled to 300. Eventually, the town died.

## What It Is Like Today

Encampment today, is a small resort and trading center for nearby dude ranches and has a population of approximately 500 year-round residents.

## Remaining Buildings

There are remnants of abandoned cabins and some old buildings.

## How To Get There

Encampment is in Carbon County.

---

### Juicy Piece of History

One of the familiar characters around the community at this time was the smelter boss, Boney Earnest. Wearing a bright red bandana around his neck, he was known to everyone. In later years, when he took to guiding visiting royalty on hunt parties, he continued to knot the gaudy handkerchief, saying it was his good luck charm.

---

# 39

# Jeffrey City

## History

Jeffrey City has an unusual tale of a ghost town. Rather than gold or silver, the town owed its prosperity to Uranium. Originally called "Home on the Range," this town was renamed for Charles W. Jeffrey. Jeffrey City's origin was the atomic bomb. It became a center of uranium production in the 1960s when Western Nuclear Corporation started operations here. The company employed hundreds of workers, but by 1980, the market for yellowcake uranium had dropped drastically, and the $50 million processing mill closed.

Besides uranium, this area was known for its jade. In 1943, Verla James found a piece of raw jade weighing 3,366 pounds. James later found other chunks totaling some 7,000 pounds. By 1945, Wyoming led the nation in jade production. Rock hunters also found Onyxed moss agates in abundance.

Jeffrey City has an eerie aura about it, quite ghostly, and still occupied by a handful of people.

## What It Is Like Today

There are only a few families loyal to Jeffrey City nowadays. It is a modern ghost town. Visitors can get a glimpse of a stray cat peeping through the windows of an old trailer occupied by a wayfaring traveler. The buildings are closed and a handful of houses are occupied. The town's once-modern duplex apartments and miners' dormitories sit boarded up on weed-choked streets. Several years ago, its entire K-12 school system closed, leaving more vacant buildings, including a colossal multi-million dollar Reagan-era gymnasium that now languishes alone on the vast rangeland.

## Remaining Buildings

Remaining Buildings include an abandoned post office, youth hostel, and the old mission house. There is also the church, now taken over by shrubs, lying next to the liquor store. Many buildings remain, closed and in poor condition.

## How To Get There

Jeffrey City is in Fremont County. From Casper, Wyoming, follow Wyoming Highway 220 West 71 miles to Muddy Gap. Turn right on U.S. 287 West for 23 miles.

## Juicy Piece of History

As mentioned, Jeffrey City had its beginnings in Uranium and the atomic bomb. With the end of the cold war, no one wanted Wyoming uranium anymore. Thus, almost no one wanted Jeffrey City. The once booming town withered and the modular homes that rolled in during the blast of productions left on flatbeds, headed for some other boomtown.

# 40

# Miner's Delight

## History

Miner's Delight was among the state of Wyoming's first communities. Gold was discovered here in 1868 and with that discovery came an era of gold mining and the establishment of the town of Hamilton City.

The town got its start at about the same time as its sister mining camps of Atlantic City and South Pass City. Gold was first discovered here in 1867 and within no time a mining camp sprang up.

However, because the largest and most productive mine, located on Peabody Hill, was called Miners Delight, most people called the town by the same name.

One resident noted in his diary: "The society in Miner's Delight consisted of three females. One he described as a "plump, dumpling-faced woman built very much in the shape of a bale of cotton drawn together in the middle, and with a big coal scuttle on the top." Of the second woman he wrote "I don't know who or what she does. The third he thought had a lean, spotty and unhealthy looking face, and the upper part of her form is like an old whale bone umbrella not properly folded."

Miner's Delight went through boom-bust periods, like many of the western mining towns did. The Miners Delight Mine first shut down in 1874, but soon reopened, only to shut down again in 1882. By the 1880s a new era of economic prosperity had dawned. Smaller booms occurred in 1907 and 1910 and then again during the Great Depression. The town was inhabited as late as 1960.

Miner's Delight was one of the homes of Calamity Jane. She came as a deserted child to Miner's Delight during its first year. Shortly after Calamity had settled in the community, a woman took her to New York to be "properly brought up." A year later she was back, thoroughly educated and in business for herself. However, Calamity Jane did not stay long in Miner's Delight. She moved to Atlantic City, where she operated a dance hall.

## What It Is Like Today

Today, Miner's Delight provides ruins of its prosperous past.

## Remaining Buildings

On the town site are structures including seven cabins, one saloon, one meat house, one shop or barn, one shaft house, one pantry, one cellar, and a corral.

# How To Get There

Situated just a few miles east of Atlantic City, Wyoming, in Fremont County.

## Juicy Piece of History

The story goes, in 1869, a man named William Jones, while chasing his cows about pasture, stumbled across some quartz with gold flecks dotting it. The site was so remote and so far above town that he erroneously assumed no one else would ever find it. Content, he continued on his way, gathering his stray cattle. When he returned to the site of the gold lode he found others working the claim. He tried to relate his tale of the discovery to the other miners but in vain. Those were the mining roots of Miner's Delight.

# 41

# Old Trail Town

## History

Old Trail Town is an assemblage of historic buildings. They include a trapper's cabin, a trading post, a stage station, and a saloon arranged along a sagebrush street.

## What It Is Like Today

The buildings are visible from the Highway, running through Cody. However, to get a closer glimpse and to walk through the town, visitors must go to the site. Tickets are $8 per person at this writing.

## Remaining Buildings

The Old Trail Town collection now consists of 26 buildings, which date from 1879 to 1901, 100 horse-drawn vehicles, plus an extensive collection of Native American artifacts and memorabilia of the Wyoming frontier.

## How To Get There

Old Trail Town is located in Cody, Wyoming, gateway to Yellowstone Park's East entrance, one mile west of Cody off Route 14/16/20.

Old Trail Town in Cody, Wyoming.

## Juicy Piece of History

Old Trail Town interprets the American West and Wyoming's colorful western past with its buildings and extensive collection of treasured memorabilia reflecting life on the Wyoming Frontier as well as the lives of many of Wyoming's colorful historical figures. These include John Johnston, Jim White "Buffalo Hunter," Phillip Vitter, a trapper killed by a grizzly bear, and W.A. Gallagher and Blind Bill, cowboys murdered in 1894.

# 42

# Shoshoni

## History

Shoshoni, was established in 1905. For a while Shoshoni was producing Uranium. The demand for impure Wyoming Uranium was slim. Soon, it dwindled. But signs of town pride resurface annually, as Shoshoni plays host to the State fiddle championships.

## What It Is Like Today

Nowadays, barely a store front survives along the dusty main street of Shoshoni. It is still home to about 635 people. The signboard at the onset of town reads "Welcome to Shoshone: Hope for the lodge."

## Remaining Buildings

This is a modern ghost town. The remaining buildings are more contemporary.

## How To Get There

South of Thermopolis. Shoshone is in Fremont County. Bonneville and Shoshoni are neighbors, about 3 miles apart.

### Juicy Piece of History

Shoshoni is a sleepy town, deteriorating in the Wyoming landscape. A few people continue to live there, but the town by itself is slowly getting claimed by Mother Nature.

# 43

# South Pass City

## History

The clear and rushing creek called Sweetwater figured prominently in early mining days. Gold had been found in the area as early as 1842. Here, the early pioneer-prospectors panned, while Indians watched from the rocks above. The White man muddied up the Indians' drinking water with his placerings and killed their food supply. The Indians didn't like it.

Retaliation came swiftly and often, but when the Indians rode into the now good-sized town of South Pass City, they found no women or children to carry off. What they didn't know was that a lookout was kept on the hill at all times, and at the approach of Indians, the women and children were herded into a cell behind the wine cellar.

The South Pass City area came in for its share of unscrupulous and desperate White characters. One instance of inhumanity occurred in 1864 when the owner of a well equipped, eight mule outfit became ill. His traveling companions, thinking him about to die, dumped him by the roadside and made off within his wagons and animals. The station tenders rescued him and nursed him back to health. A year later, the recovered victim learned the California whereabouts of the culprits. He buckled on his shooting irons and set out after them. It was reported that he found them, and since his six guns were still hot from practicing on the Sioux, the offenders never pulled another stunt.

Miners returning from California looked for Gold all over the Rockies, and in 1867, the rich Carissa Lode in Wyoming's Sweetwater district prompted a gold rush. The rushers swelled South Pass City to 2,000 citizens within a year. Even the town's two doctors moonlighted as miners.

By 1868, Wyoming's City of Gold boasted over 250 buildings. By 1870, the town had a population of 4,000 and a long main street with good shops. Numerous saloons, stamp mills, hotels, and businesses took advantage of the gold-driven economy. It had general stores, butcher shops, restaurants, clothing stores, sporting good stores, saloons, and seven different hotels. Several banks were waiting in South Pass City for the prospectors who were lucky enough to strike gold. For the rough and rowdy citizens of the old west, the jail on the south end of town was an absolute necessity. High on a hill, east of town, was a small, one-room school house. The South Pass City cemetery was located on a rise just west of town.

An old man in South Pass City said, "The ladies liked to have the latest Paris hats just like they do now. Only in those days it took a lot longer to get the hats out there. But then they stayed in style a lot longer, too. It was in such a remote location that the hats would certainly linger for a while.

It was Wyoming's good fortune that Mrs. Morris had been selected for the trial run of Woman Suffrage. She cast the pattern for successful participation in politics by the women of the state, and through it all, she kept her sense of balance and humor. Judge Esther Morris presided over thirty-four cases. Among them were intent to kill, assault and battery, and theft cases. Her original journal discloses one case where the accused stated that "believing that I cannot get a fair and unbiased trial at Atlantic City, I seek a change of venue to South Pass." Mrs. Morris decided the case involving this alleged offender.

"Mine was a test of woman's ability to hold office," Mrs. Morris modestly stated, "and during it all, I do not know that I have neglected my family any more than in ordinary shopping." To this great and motherly woman, Wyoming owes the word "Equality" which appears on the state seal.

By 1870, South Pass City had 4,000 inhabitants and by the end of 1873, it was deserted. A bust hit the area in 1872. The miners became discouraged by the lack of large gold deposits. In 1875, less than 100 people remained in the area. Within a decade the city's population shrank dramatically as the large gold deposits that had been hoped for failed to materialize.

Though South Pass City was short lived, during its life, the Carissa mine produced millions of dollars in gold and made a handful of people very wealthy. A few businesses continued to operate in South Pass City with the last of the pioneer families finally moving on in 1949. The post office closed in 1948, although the postman delivers mail to its seven residents as of August 2009.

## What It Is Like Today

South Pass City's current population is 7. The town is at an elevation of 7,905. South Pass City has been restored beautifully and is a true ghost town. Visitors can walk through old buildings and get a glimpse of life during the mining days. The city today consists of two areas: South Pass City, in which a handful of residents live, and South Pass City State Historic Site, which preserves more than 20 historic structures dating from the city's heyday in the 1860s and 1870s.

A postman still delivers mail to the residents. There is a general mercantile store and a few inhabited houses. A beautiful stream runs through the town. Tourists make the extra effort to visit South Pass City. It is in a beautiful but remote location. Accessible by any vehicle, although on rainy days and during the winter the road might require a four wheel drive.

## Remaining Buildings

Visitors can take a tour through the town. Here are some of the other remaining buildings at South Pass City:

The Blacksmith Shop, built in 1915, contained a forge and tools to repair wagons and horse-drawn equipment. It was built of logs.

The Carissa Saloon dates to the 1890s and operated sporadically until 1949.

The Carr Butcher Shop dates back to the early 1900s. William Carr operated the butcher shop. Animals were killed and quartered at his corral in Slaughterhouse Gulch, about two miles south of town, and then processed at the shop.

E.A. Slack Cabin was owned by E.A. Slack, Esther Morriss' son. He published his newspaper the *South Pass News* and lived in this house beginning in 1871.

The Cave (Fort Bourbon) is an interior stone wall built in 1868 to protect perishable food and liquor. Folklore says when townspeople feared Indian attacks, women and children were locked safely in the back while the men went out to fight.

The Libby House was built by Harry Libby in the spring of 1899 after he was dismissed by Carissa Mine superintendent. The building may have been used in 1901 as a pest house or "isolation hospital" during a small pox outbreak. It is the oldest remaining hospital in Wyoming. This building was the last on the way out of town; people either got well and walked home, or were carried up the hill to the cemetery.

Reniker Cabin belonged to William Reniker, a Civil War veteran, who lived in this cabin when not working his gold mine on Reniker Peak, northwest of town.

The Idaho House or South Pass Hotel, opened as the Idaho House in 1868, and was the finest in town.

# How To Get There

Atlantic City and South Pass City are about 2 miles apart.

# Juicy Piece of History

Just like many towns founded as a result of a gold discovery, South Pass City's early success was followed by a large exodus of people, some discouraged by the low returns and hard work in an extremely harsh winter climate, while others were lured away by rumors of bigger and brighter discoveries elsewhere. A "gold rush" did not occur until July 1867, when newspaper accounts picked up the discovery of the Carissa Lode.

In 1869 Esther McQuigg Morris, began her campaign in South Pass for equal rights for women. The Mother of Woman Suffrage in Wyoming (as she has since been called) had taken a stand for female equality.

Orphaned at the age of eleven, she had acquired a small fortune as a businesswoman. When her husband, Artemas Slack, a wealthy railroad contractor, had died in Illinois, she had been subjected to unjust property laws. She fought courageously, but unsuccessfully, for her claims as a widow. It was then that she pledged herself to work for the betterment of womankind.

Now arriving with her two sons to join her merchant husband John Morris, and her oldest son, Edward Slack, at South Pass, there still rang in her ears the challenge issued by her brother when she left Illinois: "You will never live to see the day women vote."

During the election campaign in the little mining town tucked away in the folds of the Rockies, Mrs. Morris staged her historic tea party. For her tea party, she invited interested voters and the candidates for the Territorial Council. Over the brew she extracted from the politicians the promise that whoever won would introduce a bill giving women the privilege to vote and hold office.

It became a law when Governor John A. Campbell signed it and the newborn Territory set an unprecedented and world-wide record of unique importance in that its women were the first to be freed from the masculine tutelage to which law, religion, tradition, and custom had bound them. Women were thrilled. The eyes of the world were focused upon South Pass in 1870 when Mrs. Morris was appointed the first woman Justice of the Peace and in so doing, became the first woman to hold political office in the United States. Her son, Edward Slack, Clerk of the Court, swore her to the office. These events ultimately set the stage for women's suffrage in the U.S., with the passage of the Nineteenth Amendment in 1920.

# 44

# Tensleep

## History

Tensleep is a small ranching community which represents a true example of western lifestyle. The town grew from one cabin erected in 1882. Located at the base of the Big Horn Mountains, the area is rich in fertile soil and waterways, which makes it perfect for raising cattle and sheep.

During Wyoming's range feud of the late 1800s, cattlemen near Tensleep opposed sheep grazing for two reasons: Cattle already overstocked the land, and the cowmen believed sheep ruined the range. Cattlemen eventually realized they might make a profit by raising sheep themselves and some began to import the animals. One of the first to do so in the Big Horn Basin was Joe Emge. In 1909 he brought in 5,000 sheep. They had barely turned the animals loose on the range when seven armed men attacked.

Officials launched a grand jury investigation that almost perpetuated the violence. The incident at Tensleep finally brought the situation to a head: Sheepmen and cattlemen would have to share the range. The cattlemen no longer had control.

In the 1920s and 1930s, the graded road east of Tensleep was not for the faint-hearted. The Tensleep Canyon was very dangerous. For travelers heading east, the gas stations, cafe, and hotel at the town of Tensleep, were literally a "last chance stop."

The area is full of history and is recognized as being the site of many historic battlegrounds between Indian tribes and the white man. Among those sites are the Bates Battlesite, an engagement in which the Arapahoe were defeated by a coalition composed of U.S. troops and the Shoshone.

## What It Is Like Today

Scenic wonders ranging from mountain ranges, canyons, pure mountain streams and lakes are everywhere. Expect to see abundant sightings of elk, moose, deer, and other forest creatures.

## Remaining Buildings

The Tensleep Museum displays local artifacts, fossils, rocks, pioneer clothing, and farm and household equipment. The Mountain Man Café occupies one of the town's original business buildings from the early 1900s.

# How To Get There

Travelers from the east will embark on the Big Horn Mountains via Cloud Peak Sky (U.S. Hwy. 16) after exiting the I-90 corridor in Buffalo. Tensleep and Worland are next to each other.

## Juicy Piece of History

Tensleep received its name because of the method of measuring distance that was used by Indians at one time. There was once a large Sioux Indian camp on the banks of the Platte River, and there was another large Indian camp on the Clark's Fork River to the North, near present-day Bridger, Montana. These camps were important to Indians and settlers due to the trails leading to and from them in all directions across the West. According to the reckoning of the Indians, it was ten "sleeps," or nights, between the two camps.

During the struggle for grazing rights between cattle and sheep ranchers from 1897 to 1909 the Tensleep area was the site of a notorious raid when masked night riders swooped down on a sheep camp on Spring Creek. In 1903, they killed two sheep owners and a herder, then set fire to a wagon to incinerate the bodies. The event eventually led to the end of the bitter rivalry between cattlemen and sheep ranchers. The Sheepmen Burial Site located seven and a half miles south of TenSleep on Route 434 is the location of a marker and the graves from the raid.

# 45

# Thermopolis

## History

In 1898, the town of Thermopolis was organized. It was well known for its healing waters. Early treaties show that the mineral spa was no gift. There was a long and drawn out dispute between the government and the Shoshone and Arapaho tribes for the rights to the steaming bath tubs. Thermopolis has the world's largest mineral hot springs.

## What It Is Like Today

Thermopolis lies in the spot where the Wind River changes its name as it tumbles out of Wind River Canyon to become the Big Horn . At one time, Thermopolis was the site of an Indian reservation, the northeast corner of the Shoshone. Today, it is a vibrant town, with a population living year round.

## Remaining Buildings

The remaining buildings are mostly modern ones. The museum lies on the main road. St. Francis Catholic Church is a historic building.

## How To Get There

Thermopolis lies 150 miles from the East Gate of Yellowstone National Park.

### Juicy Piece of History

Said Chief Washakie, reduced to bartering his favorite warm springs. "I always thought of the land as belonging to me, but I think now that somebody always gets ahead of me. My land is pretty large and I have not stolen it. My friends that spoke for and secured this land are all dead and gone. I am the only one of the old men of my people left. I came here and stayed. I have been poor a long while. I would like each tribe to get $30,000. I want to keep one spring for myself and my people, but I will sell the others." The treaty negotiated in 1896 made no mention of a spring for the tribes.

# 46

# Worland

## History

A genial man named C.H. Worland set up camp along the Bridger Trail to the Montana gold country in about 1900, building a post office and stage station. The settlement that grew here was called Camp Worland. C.H. Worland, better known as "Dad" Worland sold seedlings for the Start Nursery Company of Missouri when he saw the possibilities of the land at the mouth of Fifteen Mile Creek.

The town of Worland has always depended on the land. Boasting one of the state's longest growing seasons and the warmest temperatures in the summer, Worland has a deep and varied agricultural background. C.H. Worland took advantage of this. In 1900, he claimed a homestead. Then he obtained a supply of whisky and opened the Hole-in-the-Wall as a stop on the stage route midway between Basin and Thermopolis.

As an agricultural salesman, Worland recognized the importance of deep rich soil. He also recognized that without water it had little production value. However, the Big Horn River ran through the area, and in 1903, the Lincoln Land Company started efforts to develop a canal and irrigation system. Worland persuaded engineers to select a location near his homestead for a town site.

The town consisted of "Dad" Worland's Saloon, two hotels, dance hall, a tent school house, three retail stores, four residences, a Chinese Laundry and the Hanover Canal Company Office. The rail road got extended to Worland.

In later years, B.C. Buffum took samples of emmer wheat to Worland. He farmed some land himself and shared the seeds with others. By 1909, Buffum had built a cereal factory, making a product called Emmer Food. Although popular with the residents, the factory operated only a few years. Buffum closed it because of either failing health or failing finances, or a combination of the two.

Closure of the factory left farmers in search of a new cash crop. Eventually they turned to alfalfa.

On November 10, 1907, a fire swept through Worland, destroying half of the city.

In 1918, a sugar beet factory opened. Since that time, sugar beets have been the primary cash crop in the region. The Wyoming Sugar Company became Holly Sugar Company in the 1920s and is the oldest sugar processing mill in Wyoming. As sugar beets became the biggest crop raised in the Big Horn Basin, the rural population grew with many Mexican, Russian, German, and Japanese workers and residents. By the 1980s, farmers had expanded to other crops including beans and a number of feedlot operations located near Worland as well.

# What It Is Like Today

Worland remains an agricultural town. It is located in a beautiful area in a colorful landscape.

# Remaining Buildings

The Washakie Museum: Earth, Science, History, and Art displays the bones of mammoths and has changing exhibitions on the region's art, history, geology, archaeology, and paleontology. The Worland House is a bungalow style house built in 1917. It belonged to Charlie Worland (Dad's son) and his wife, Sadie.

# How To Get There

Worland is right next to Tensleep.

## Juicy Piece of History

Some residents call the era from 1912-1917 the Alfalfa period. During that time, men of the community organized the Alfalfa Club. The Alfalfa Club sponsored a Washakie Days celebration that included a picnic, baseball game, and other activities.

COLORADO & SOUTHERN

Section Five

# Ghost Towns
# of Montana

# 47

# Bannack

## History

Bannack was founded in 1862 when John White discovered gold on Grasshopper Creek. As news of the gold strike spread, many prospectors and businessmen rushed to Bannack, hoping to strike it rich. A mining camp was quickly built, literally springing up overnight. Most of the miners lived in tents, caves, dugouts, huts, and wagons.

By 1863, the settlement had gained some 3,000 residents and applied to the U.S. Government for the name of Bannock, named for the neighboring Indians. However, Washington goofed it up, spelling the name with an "a," Bannack, which it retains to this day.

By May 1864, Sidney Edgerton, the territorial Chief Justice decided there were so many people in the area that they needed a new territory. Edgerton convinced the president and on May 26, 1864, it was made official, with Edgerton as the governor. Bannack became the first territorial capital and the Legislature of Montana met in Sidney Edgerton's cabin.

The people who rushed to Bannack were not only miners, they also included many deserters of the Civil War, outlaws and businessmen intent on profiting from the many newcomers. These early settlers arrived by wagon, stagecoach, horse back, steamboat, and even by foot, in search of their fortunes. Not anticipating the harsh Montana winters, many came ill-prepared and lacking supplies, creating a great hardship for these early pioneers.

Masonic Lodge members met on the second story of the Masonic Temple, which had a double floor to muffle their secret conversations; a school occupied the first story. Iron rings mounted in the floor of the Bannack Jail for chaining criminals so they could not escape through the sod roof. A bootlegger's cabin produced moonshine as recently as early 1960s.

By the fall of 1864, the town hit its peak. At its peak, Bannack had a population of about 3,000. There were three hotels, three bakeries, three blacksmith shops, two stables, two meat markets, a grocery store, a restaurant, a brewery, a billiard hall, and four saloons. Though all of the businesses were built of logs, some had decorative false fronts. Settlements were so numerous and scattered that people called the area the "fourteen-mile city." By 1870, there were no more easy diggings in Bannack, and within just a couple of years, the population of Bannack shrank to a just a few hundred.

From the late 1860s to the 1930s, Bannack continued as a mining town with a fluctuating population. By the 1950s, gold workings had dwindled and most folks had moved on. At that point, the State of Montana declared Bannack a State Park in 1954.

# What It Is Like Today

The Montana Department of Fish, Wildlife, and Parks governs the town site and the surrounding area of Bannack. Today, over sixty structures remain standing, most of which can be explored. People from all over visit this renowned ghost town to discover its heritage.

Bannack State Park is open year round. The Visitor Center is open seven days a week during the summer months.

# Remaining Buildings

Remaining Buildings include Bessette House, Spokane Mining house, Bannack jails, Gibson houses, Masonic Lodge/School house, Methodist Church, Roe/Graves house, bachelors row, Goodrich Hotel, Skinner's Saloon, and Hotel Meade. Skinner's Saloon, built in 1863 is one of the few structures surviving from the town's earliest period. Here, Sheriff Henry Plummer picked up casual information about gold shipments to relay to his cutthroat gang.

# How To Get There

In Beaverhead County, Montana, just outside of Dillon.

# Juicy Piece of History

In addition to its reputation for gold, Bannack also quickly gained a reputation for lawlessness. The roads in and out of town were home to dozens of road agents, and killings were frequent.

The stretch of road between Bannack and Virginia City was the scene of more holdups, robberies, and murders than almost any other comparable stagecoach route. About a hundred men were murdered during 1863. This murderous crew had for its mastermind the Sheriff of Bannack.

Henry Plummer was an escapee, having fled from the camps of California and Nevada. In Bannack he started life anew. To the populace, he set himself up as a preserver of the peace. In 1863, he soon became official sheriff and built the jail. He was elected sheriff in hopes that he might bring some peace to the lawless settlement. He became a symbol of hospitality, the scene of receptions and dances for the upper crust. At the same time, behind this screen of respectability, Plummer pulled the strings that ended in over a hundred murders and a bonanza of money and jewelry taken from unfortunate stagecoach travelers.

What was not known by the citizens of Bannack, was that Plummer was the leader of the largest gang of the area road agents. This group of bandits referred to themselves as the "Innocents" and grew to include more than 100 men. His contacts as sheriff gave him knowledge of when people were transporting their gold, which he would pass on to his gang. The notorious Henry Plummer was Bannack's sheriff until the vigilantes hanged him in 1864.

Plummer's masquerade as head of all useful and law abiding citizens is one of the most incredible episodes in the history of the west.

By December, 1863, the citizens of Bannack and Virginia City had had enough of the violence. Men from Bannack, Virginia City, and nearby Nevada City met secretly and organized the Montana Vigilantes. Masked men began to visit suspected outlaws in the middle of the night issuing warnings and tacking up posters featuring a skull-and-crossbones or the "mystic" numbers "3-7-77." While the meaning of these numbers remains elusive, the Montana State Highway patrolmen wear the emblem "3-7-77" on their shoulder patches even today.

The vigilantes hanged about twenty-four men. When one such man, by the name of Erastus "Red" Yager, who was about to be hanged, pointed a finger at Sheriff Henry Plummer as the leader of the gang, all hell broke loose.

On January 10, 1864, fifty to seventy-five men gathered up Plummer and his two main deputies. Plummer promised to tell the vigilantes where $100,000 of gold was buried, if they would let him live. That didn't happen. Plummer was killed.

In the meantime the vigilantes continued their antics and three years after Sheriff Plummer was hanged, the vigilantes virtually ruled the mining districts. Finally, leading citizens of Montana, including Territorial Governor Thomas Meagher, began to speak out against the ruthless group. In March 1867, the miners issued their own warning that if the vigilantes hanged any more people, the "law abiding citizens" would retaliate "five for one." Though a few more holdups occurred, the era of the vigilantes ended.

# 48

# Castle City

## History

Castle City was also known as Castletown, or just "Castle." Castle was a silver and lead-producing town. The camp got its start around 1882 when a prospector named Hanson Barnes found silver in the area.

When the ground was frozen and the Hensley brothers couldn't farm, they took off separately to "look around." There was little snow that winter, the ground was exposed during the week they were there, and one of them picked up a chunk of float which caused them to hurry to the smelter. The piece of galena was rich in lead and silver when assayed.

The discovery ridge was called Yellowstone by the Hensley brothers who now abandoned their ranch and located a group of mines on the steep slope. Outcroppings were discovered in the area as early as 1882, but little mining was done until 1884. Castletown was named after the castle-like rocks adorning nearby Castle Mountain.

The first mine built was the North Carolina Mine in 1884. Its richest producer however, was the Cumberland Mine, which began mining for lead in 1884. Before long, the company was employing numerous miners and the town boomed. The camp gave rise to some 2,000 residents, a fine school, numerous merchants, several fraternal organizations, a jail, seven brothels, and as many as fourteen saloons.

It was at this period that Calamity Jane came to Castle to run a restaurant. She had tried the restaurant business elsewhere, losing out because of drunken escapades. In Castle, she was determined to lead a circumspect life, putting on the act for the benefit of business and daughter. It didn't really work. Due to her drunken stupors, she had to give up her daughter to the Sisters of St. Martin.

There was a great deal of gambling and carousing in saloons and dancehalls, especially after payday, which was the twentieth; but strangely enough, in the entire history of Castle City there was never a fatality resulting from gunfight or other violence – many did die from frequent mine accidents, though. Although Castle had its full quota of saloons, brothels, and bawdy houses so necessary to mining camp survival, it had its refinements, too. There were social clubs, parties, dances, spelling bees, and other society affairs. Everyone expected a solid future for Castle.

Castle's major problem, however, was a lack of transportation, which required that all ore and supplies be hauled in and out by the wagon load. Although three stage lines provided daily service to four other area towns, Castle needed a railroad to haul its mail, ore, mining machinery, coke, and people. The rich ore was first hauled to the Yellowstone Mine's Smelter, more than 100 miles to the south. At one time Castle was considered one of the richest mining camps in the state. Copper king Marcus Daly invested heavily in mines in the area, as did many other capitalists.

Castle began to go down hill when silver was demonetized in 1893. People began to leave in droves for greener pastures, leaving behind those who thought they could make it by mining lead. When the price of lead dropped, the town became a ghost town.

By 1936, only two people lived in Castle: 75 year old "Mayor" Joseph Hooker Kidd and 70-year-old Constable Joseph Martino. Kidd's death was the next to the last chapter in the death of Castle. Here is what happened to them. It was a bitter winter, with snow drifts up to forty feet. Provisions were almost gone, so Kidd hitched up his team and headed for Lennep, seven miles away. The first day Kidd made only three miles, staying the night in a sheep camp. He finally made it to Lennep, got the mail and supplies and headed back. He spent the night at a ranch, and the next day managed to get within a mile of Castle before his team gave out. He walked the rest of the way arriving at 9 p.m. After a hot cup of coffee, Kidd headed for his home, 500 yards away. En route he collapsed and died. Martino was too weak to carry the body, so he covered it with a blanket. Martino made the three mile trip on skis, to the sheep camp. Three days later the sheriff and Coroner from White Sulphur Springs skied into Castle, placed Kidd's body on a toboggan, and left Joseph Martino as the last resident.

## What It Is Like Today

The old mining camp is a classic ghost town with several buildings still standing including cabins, a couple of businesses, the school, and stone foundations. Castle City is on private land and close inspection of the property requires permission. However, a public road runs near the town which provides a number of nice views.

## Remaining Buildings

There are a few stone foundations remaining, and more wooden structures off the road a ways. Some of these are in very good condition. The road goes up further into the State Park lands, where the mine that made Castle is located.

## How To Get There

The old camp is located off of Highway 294 between White Sulphur Springs and Martinsdale,

# Juicy Piece of History

One story is told about a new undertaker in Castle. A man in poor circumstances had been killed in an explosion in a mine. A collection was taken up for the widow and a nice funeral which included a suit of clothes for the victim. After the service the undertaker suggested postponing burial until the day following as the road up the hill might be less icy. One curious individual, wondering why another day might be better when it froze every night, slipped in the back door of the "parlor" next to the furniture store and caught the undertaker removing the new suit from the body.

Probably the best-known one time resident of Castle City was Calamity Jane. Born in Princeton, Missouri, on May 1, 1852, as Martha Cannary, she grew up to look and act like a man. They say she could shoot like a cowboy, drink like a fish, and exaggerate the tales of her life to any and all who would listen.

In 1870, she joined General George Armstrong Custer as a scout at Fort Russell, Wyoming. This was the beginning of Calamity Jane's habit of dressing like a man.

An interesting incident took place at Goose Creek, Wyoming. Captain Egan was in command of the Post and the troops were ordered out to quell an Indian uprising. Captain Egan was the first to be shot and fell from his horse. Galloping back, Calamity Jane lifted him onto her horse and got him safely back to the Fort. Captain Egan on recovering, laughingly said, "I name you Calamity Jane, the heroine of the plains."

Calamity Jane came to Castle to open a restaurant determined to lead a lady-like existence. With her was a little girl, a daughter of one of her many husbands. Such was not to be. She eventually returned to the boomtown of Deadwood in the Black Hills where she was welcomed "home" but continued to be the Calamity Jane everyone had come to know.

# 49

# Comet

## History

Mining began in Comet in what would become known as the High Ore Mining District as early as 1869 when a man named John W. Russell began to prospect in the area. However, after working his claim for five years, Russell sold it to the Alta-Montana Company in 1874. The new company began to invest in mining operations and soon built a 40-ton-per-day concentrator, a mill process which separates the ore from the dirt and rocks.

The town reportedly sported twenty-two saloons at one time. Unofficial estimates put the number of pupils attending the Comet School in 1930 at twenty, with a total mill-mine employment figure of 300.

However, by the turn of the century, the ore was beginning to play out and the mine sold several times over the next several years. By 1913, the town had become a ghost town.

Things changed again in 1927, when the Comet and the Gray Eagle Mines were purchased by the Basin Montana Tunnel Company, who again made improvements, building a 200-ton concentrator, which was described at the time as "the most modern in Montana." With better technology, the mines were buzzing once again, employing about 300 men and weathering the depression years. The mine finally closed when the United States entered World War II and the townspeople left. Mining operations continued until 1941, at which time, most of the equipment was sold, the people moved away, and Comet became a ghost town for good.

## What It Is Like Today

Today, the town sits silent, crumbling amongst the sagebrush and weeds. Though Mother Nature and years of vandalism have taken a toll on the old town, more than two dozen buildings continue to stand, testifying to more prosperous times.

## Remaining Buildings

The town's most prominent structure, the Dailey Hotel, is now closely wrapped by an aspen grove. The giant Comet mine still stands. On a hillside, stands a simple, L-shaped wooden house, where members of one of Comet's early families, the Mattsons, lived.

## How To Get There

Comet is located about 37 miles southwest of Helena, Montana. Travel south of Helena on I-15 to Exit 160. Travel north on High Ore Road for about five miles.

### Juicy Piece of History

In 1885, the greater Comet area was home to 300 residents and contained approximately 90 buildings. The Comet Mine was profitable through the rest of the decade and the 1890s, weathering the silver panic and depression of 1893. The mine was sold several times in the early 1900s. Although most precious metals had been mined out by then, the mine continued to produce valuable lead, zinc, and iron.

During these prosperous years, the Comet School had at least twenty children attending. The town has twenty-two saloons. At Rosie's Boardinghouse, miners who commonly received $3.90 per shift could find room and board for 75 cents a day.

# 50

# Coolidge

## History

Mining began when rich veins of silver were discovered high in the Pioneer Mountains in 1872 by a man named Preston Sheldon. The claim was called the "Old Elkhorn" because a pair of elk horns had been found near the discovery site. As more prospectors began to flood the area, dozens of claims and mines began operations. However, the work was severely restricted due to the lack of economical transportation.

Mining started seriously in 1911. The town had a boarding house and restaurant, as well as a company store that provided food and supplies to the residents. Amazingly, the mining camp never held a saloon, but alcohol was said to have been available from a local joint outside of the camp.

A post office was established in Coolidge in January 1922, and that same year, the new mill, covering nearly two acres, was completed at a cost of about $900,000. This was the largest mill in Montana. It had the capacity to process 750 tons of ore per day with a recovery rate of 90%-93%. Initially, many miners lived in tents, which were later replaced by more substantial log buildings. The town was bustling with activity at this point. There was access to telephone services and electricity.

However, by the time the mining operations had been fully developed, it was already beginning to struggle as silver prices plummeted and the national economy took a downturn in 1893.

The miners and their families began to move away. By 1932, the vast majority of the townspeople were gone and the post office was discontinued.

## What It Is Like Today

Today, the town is deserted. Most of its buildings are tumbling to the ground. Today, the site is located within the Beaverhead Deerlodge National Forest.

## Remaining Buildings

Many structures including large mines remain. Though dozens of buildings continue to stand, they are quickly being reclaimed by Mother Nature.

## How To Get There

Coolidge is located south of Butte, Montana. From I-15, travel west on SR-43, then south onto NF-73 (Wise River Polaris Road), then east down a dirt road. It then requires about a ½ mile hike to the old town site.

## Juicy Piece of History

There were a few spurts of mining activity, but it was not until 1911 that Coolidge became successful. In 1911, a Montana politician named William R. Allen also began buying claims, and in 1913, formed the Boston Montana Mining Company. After investigating the claims, the company began efforts to reopen the Elkhorn Mine, and the following year, the town of Coolidge was born, named after William Allen's friend, Calvin Coolidge.

o

# 51

# Elkhorn

## History

Elkhorn was once a prosperous mining town that produced silver ore and gold. Rich silver deposits were first discovered here by a Swiss immigrant by the name of Peter Wyes in 1870. Wyes did not live to enjoy its rewards, as he died mysteriously after a few years of his discovery. In 1875, a Norwegian man named Anton M. Holter entered the picture. He had already made a name for himself as an entrepreneur and mining mogul. Holter acquired Wyles' claim and developed what was at first called the Holter lode. Before long word got out of the rich silver ores to be mined in the area.

The town had stores, fourteen saloons, several churches, and lodge halls. Transportation was next to impossible and only the barest necessities came in for a long time, but in 1889, the Northern Pacific drove a line up to the 5,500-foot-high city, running in three trains a week.

In the 1880s, Elkhorn reached its peak, supporting a population of about 2,500 people, with many more living in the surrounding gulches. Lining Main Street were three hotels, a post office, a bowling alley, four ice houses, several retail stores, a barber shop, blacksmith livery, and numerous saloons. The town also had a Methodist church, and hundreds of homes, cabins, and boarding houses.

Everything that comes along with mining was brought to Elkhorn: disease, homicide, mining and woodcutting, accidents, supply problems, fires, brutal hours of work, saloons, prostitution, and gambling.

In May 1893, work began on a new Fraternity Hall for the town to serve as a social center. Built in a modified Greek revival architectural style, the Fraternity Hall still stands today. The two-story building featured a large hall on its first floor and a large meeting room on the second.

By the time the Fraternity Hall was completed, however, Elkhorn's population had already fallen dramatically to about 600. The mining began to taper off, but the Elkhorn Mine continued operations full time until 1900.

## What It Is Like Today

Elkhorn has been dead for many years. Though it still has a few remaining residents this small town today is a far cry from the beehive of activity it displayed over a century ago. On both sides of the street straggle lines of old and weathered buildings. Today, the preserved Fraternity Halland Gilian Hall are part of the smallest state park in Montana and are open for visitors. All other properties in the old mining camp are on private property and occupied. The cemetery has stone and wooden markers spanning a century. Markers at head and foot are common, as are metal and wooden paling fences surrounding grave sites.

## Remaining Buildings

The Fraternity Hall remains in Elkhorn. The Fraternity Brothers Hall is considered to be one of the most historically significant western American structures still standing. The Grand Hotel remains as well.

## How To Get There

Elkhorn is located just 8 miles northwest of Boulder, Montana.

## Juicy Piece of History

Unlike many other gold camps that were called home to large groups of single rowdy men, Elkhorn's residents primarily comprised of European immigrant families who not only worked in the mines, but also were woodcutters in the forest.

Various lodge meetings were held upstairs of the Fraternity Hall as well as community events such as talent shows, dances, concerts, and traveling theater productions. Outdoor social events were also popular such as horse races, rock drilling contests, baseball games, town picnics, and skating parties.

The historic cemetery can also be viewed, which unfortunately holds the graves of dozens of children who died in 1888 and 1889 as a result of a harsh winter and diphtheria epidemic. The markers tell of a diphtheria epidemic which claimed the lives of many infants and children.

# 52

# Garnet

## History

The gold mines that gave rise to the town of Garnet were hard-rock mines that demanded entrepreneurs with access to industrial equipment. The town and the entire mountain range near it were named from the Brown garnet rock found there, used as an abrasive and a semi precious stone. Hundreds of miners brought their families to live at the top of the long, steep grade. The men worked hard, without electricity, with only steam engines and hand tools to aid them. The miners removed gold, silver, and copper.

F.A. Davy operated the Garnet General Store for forty-five years. He was not popular with the children of the town. Occasionally, the children would order candy from him and pay him in rocks. They hanged him in effigy from the flagpole of the hotel and you can still see some ragged remains of the stingy merchant's proxy hanging there. Mr. Davy also ran the Garnet Stage Line and Garnet Freight Line.

There were about fifty mines in the area. Placer miners were active in the area as early as the 1860s and placer gold was found in the First Chance Gulch in 1865. It was not until an abundance of gold was discovered at the Nancy Hanks Mine in 1898 that Garnet became a boomtown.

The sharp switchbacks and steep approach to Garnet are called the "Chinee" Grade. The story is that a Chinese miner hid a sizable fortune there, concealed in a five-pound baking powder can. It has never been found.

The population of Garnet grew and it was much more of a community than typical mining towns. In 1898, there were 1,200 people living in Garnet. There was daily stagecoach transportation and supplies were available in Missoula and Deer Lodge, just a three-day's journey from Garnet.

There were hotels, saloons, stores, a school, a Chinese laundry and barbershops. It was a fun-loving community that enjoyed dances, theater, harvest festivals and union meetings. There were parties, picnics, fishing trips, and a social life for its residents. The town was a union town, with a strong miners' union, the Garnet Western Labor Union, negotiating with mine owners for fair pay, working hours, and safety rules. Drinking, gambling, and prostitution were present, as in many other mining towns, but controlled to a great degree. The jail was available as an incentive to keep rowdy drunkenness to a minimum.

Garnet had harsh winters. It was during one of those winters that the snow came down so hard and so long that supplies ran out. When things began to get really desperate, one brave individual put on his miner's light, went down into the maze of shafts and tunnels, and made his way through one connection after another until he had gone the whole eleven miles to the next town and arranged supplies to be sent up. And his is one page in Montana ghost town lore which shines brightly in contrast to tarnished records of greed and cruelty which often permeates the history of these settlements.

During its heyday, Garnet boasted the Garnet Hotel. Insurance agent John H. Cole, at the News Office, was advertising weekly in *The Garnet Mining News* his bonds, leases, and deeds, or other legal papers. E.C. Lewis, proprietor of the Mascot Saloon, was proclaiming: "Just opened, with everything new, clean, and bright."

But, by 1905, the gold was playing out and only 150 people remained. A raging fire took place in 1912. Half the town was burnt and never re-built. World War I made things even more difficult. Most of the remaining miners, wives, and children left the town. Employment opportunities presented by World War I attracted remaining residents away. Garnet slowly slipped into obscurity, despite a brief renewal of mining in the Great Depression of the 1930s.

The Nancy Hank Mine continued to work on and off, until 1954. Between the years of 1897 and 1917, $950,000 had been produced, 95% of which was gold; the remaining was copper and silver. By 1960, the Montana School of Mines declared the mine dead, unprofitable.

As recently as 1948, the town came to life for a few hours. Davey auctioned gold pans, harnesses, clothing, laces, high-button shoes, miners' tools and other items from his store supplies.

# What It Is Like Today

Garnet has an isolated feel to it and is not heavily toured or commercialized.

# Remaining Buildings

Today, several buildings remain, including a log and frame cabin, a store, a saloon, and the remains of the J. K. Wells Hotel. There are also several miners' cabins still standing. A Visitor's Center is located on site featuring books and gift items and interpretive signs and self-guided trails explain the historic site.

# How To Get There

Located in the mountains of Granite County, Montana, about 45 miles east of Missoula.

# Juicy Piece of History

Garnet came alive the first time in 1862 as a gold mining town. Here, the snow comes down like white corn flakes and in no time is ten feet deep. Garnet's wealth was in gold and they took millions out in the years following the original discoveries in 1862. There would have been even more but so many of the men were too drunk to work much of the time. The mine that turned out the richest, the "Nancy Hanks," was owned by two partners, one of whom was much addicted to alcohol. After one protracted spree the other partner bought him out for $50. In the several years following, the "Nancy Hanks" spewed out $10,000,000 in gold. The retired partner had moved down to Beartown and one day, when another load of rich ore from the mine rolled past his door he hanged himself.

Kelly's Saloon is believed to be haunted. Sounds of music and laughter are reportedly heard there even in the dead of winter when only one individual is overseeing the town.
Caretakers also report hearing unexplained footsteps in the old Wells Hotel, as well as doors shutting even in places where no doors are present. Whether it's the Saloon or the hotel, those who've experienced the unexplained phenomena confirm that as soon as you approach the building, the noises immediately stop.

Garnet was mostly left to the memories and the ghosts when the town's remaining merchant, Frank Davey, died in 1947.

# 53

# Laurin

## History

Laurin is pronounced locally as "Lauray." Laurin was established in 1863 around a trading post run by a Frenchman named Jean Baptiste Laurin. The first strikes occurred in 1863. The settlement was first called Cicero, but later renamed for the Frenchman. Jean Baptiste Laurin. He bought up much of the surrounding agricultural land. Together with his wife he operated the mercantile and ranched in the area for almost four decades.

Jean Baptiste Laurin was only five feet, seven inches tall. Some reports estimate his weight at near 350 pounds. Although he could neither read nor write, he was a shrewd businessman and one estimate is that he built an economic empire valued at about $500,000. One report indicates that at one time he owned all the stores, bridges, and most of the ranches, cattle, horses, and mules for a hundred miles along the valley. His stores carried canned fruits and vegetables, groceries, a few dry goods, prepared cocktails, robes, and skins. Laurin was also a money lender, charging anywhere from twelve to thirty-six percent for unsecured loans.

Laurin and his wife prospered tremendously in the town, building an empire. They improved the town immensely, and built several stores, land, and a money-lending business. But, they were also generous. They adopted several area children. The Laurins built the Catholic church in 1901 that still stands today.

The town began to profit from the many riches of Alder Gulch, as it became a supply center for area miners and fur trappers. The supply center soon boasted several retail businesses, a post office, a hotel, saloons, and an ice cream parlor.

## What It Is Like Today

Today, Laurin still has some of the old relics of its early years amid buildings of a more modern time. It sleeps as a quiet little community.

## Remaining Buildings

Laurin has several historic buildings including the old schoolhouse, which is now a private residence, the old Morse Bros. Mercantile, the 1901 St. Mary Assumption Church, picturesque barns, and more.

# How To Get There

Laurin is in Madison County, Montanna.

## Juicy Piece of History

On January 4, 1864, Laurin gained notoriety when two road agents named Erastus "Red" Yager and George Brown were hanged from a cottonwood tree that still stands outside of Laurin. They were members of the Plummer gang.

Perhaps the most interesting structure left in Laurin is the St. Mary's Assumption Church. Father Giorda was the priest at Virginia City. The church received a bell which Father Giorda had purchased in St. Louis and had shipped up the Missouri River to Fort Benton then hauled to Virginia City by wagon. The 400-pound brass bell was cast in 1848. In 1930, when Virginia City was razed, the residents began to attend the Saint Mary's Assumption Church built in Laurin in 1901.

# 54
# Virginia City

## History

Virginia City quickly developed into one of the prominent cities of the Rocky Mountains. At its peak, 10,000 people flooded the area, which was named "Fourteen-mile City" for the numerous settlements that lined the Alder Gulch area. In 1864, the Montana Territory was carved out of Idaho Territory. Within a year, Congress created the Territory of Montana and Virginia City became the largest settlement.

Virginia City became the site of many "firsts" in Montana's colorful history. Among which were: the first transportation hub, the first newspaper (the *Montana Post*), the first meeting of the Montana Historical Society, the first public school, and Montana's first Masonic Lodge. The actual buildings associated with many of these historic events remain preserved, and provide an extraordinary glimpse into the architecture and daily life of the 1860s.

By 1875, the town began to experience a decline. By that time the most easily accessible gold from placer mining had been exploited and development and population in the territory was moving towards Helena. Most of the Gulch camps had been abandoned and Virginia City's population was less than 800 people; approximately forty percent of whom were Chinese who had been diligently working abandoned claims sites for years.

One saloonkeeper "Count" Henri Murat was found to be using weighted scales to cheat his customers out of their gold dust at the bar. Despite such corruption, churches, amateur theatrical companies, and a "Literary Association" also existed in Virginia City, creating a mixture of the rough and the refined.

What made it all worthwhile, of course, was gold. The glittering dust was everywhere—Chinese laundrymen regularly panned their wash water after doing the miner's clothes, sometimes finding gold.

Gold also drew a violent, criminal element, who could operate because of the town's isolation. "Road agents" preyed on ore shipments. Traveling on the only road to Bannack meant risking one's life. When millions in gold began to pour out of the gulch, the only road to ship it over was the one to Bannack, infested by Plummer's gang of brigands. Most notorious of the outlaws was Henry Plummer, a handsome charmer who got himself installed as county sheriff. He secretly led the Innocents," a highly organized gang who recognized each other by a password "I am innocent" and a sign which was a neckerchief with a particular knot. Because of his position as a lawman, Plummer was able to learn when a rich miner or gold shipment was leaving town and so he informed his henchmen. Stealing and plundering on the ninety mile stretch between Alder Gulch and Bannack, Plummer's gang slaughtered at least 102 people in two years.

In response, a group of Masons formed the Vigilantes in 1863. The Vigilantes caught Plummer's entire gang. Plummer sobbed and begged for his life but he and two of his men were hung. The Vigilantes also hanged Boone Helm, who once dined on a human leg. As mentioned earlier, the Vigilantes often left their own mysterious symbol attached to the bodies, 3-7-77, numbers that even today appear on the shoulder patches of Montana highway patrolmen.

## What It Is Like Today

Today, Virginia City is a kind of freestanding museum, with five streets of restored and fully furnished buildings. It is a well preserved old west, Victorian gold mining town. Visitors walk the same boardwalks that desperate Vigilantes once patrolled.

## Remaining Buildings

View over 100 historic buildings complete with artifacts and furnishings. Ride the 1910 fully refurbished steam locomotive, the stagecoach, attend a live theater show, stay the night in homey historic lodging.

Many are original, dating from the 1860s and 1870s. Content Corner is a stone building built in 1864, whose second story served as capitol offices for the Montana Territory. Other buildings include a general store filled with merchandise from the 1870s, an assay office, a barbershop, two houses of ill repute, the still-functioning Madison County Courthouse of 1876, and the log and stone Vigilante Barn. The Vigilante Barn now displays wagons, buggies, and stagecoaches.

## How To Get There

20 miles west of Yellowstone National Park (90 miles by road).

# Juicy Piece of History

The date was May 26, the year 1863. It was about four o'clock in the afternoon. Bill Fairweather had been elected the leader of the group of six miners searching for gold. Bill had no trouble giving orders, and on that day, he gave one that made history. "There is a piece of bedrock projecting and we had better go over and see if we can't get enough money to buy a little tobacco." He dug enough dirt to fill a pan, sending Harry Edgar to wash it out. The spade work done, he poked around some more with a butcher's knife and found color enough to make him shout "I've found a scad." The group finished washing it and two others before it got dark. When the first pan turned up $2.40, they knew the gulch had great potential.

The prospectors fully intended to keep their discovery a deep secret, but the find must have been written all over their faces. Everyone was their friend.

What Bill had discovered would prove to be one of the richest gold deposits in North America, and would be the seminal event in the history of Montana.

Word spread like wildfire. Miners covered the hillsides with tents, brush shelters and crude, log cabins.

Between 1863 and 1889, at least $90,000,000 in gold had been extracted from Alder Gulch. Bill Fairweather died, unable to enjoy any of it. He was only 39 years old, and a penniless alcoholic.

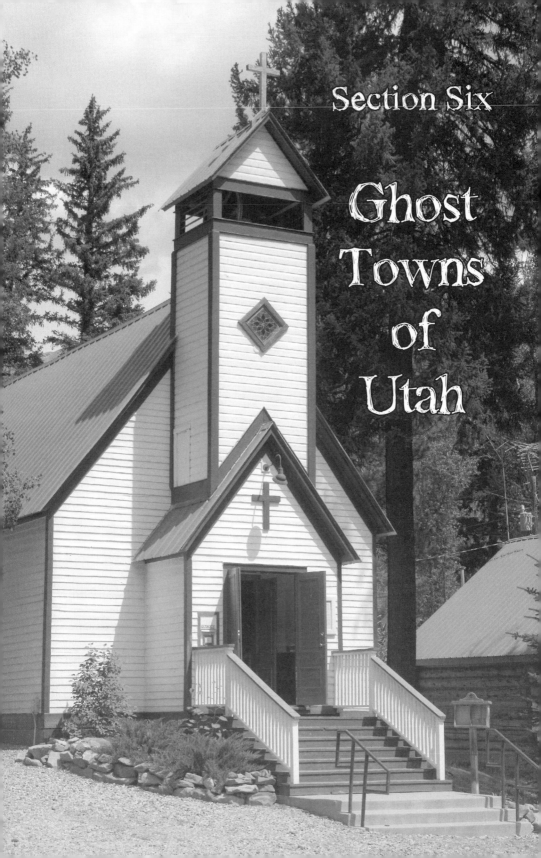

Ghost
Towns
of
Utah

# 55

# Cisco

## History

Cisco is an eerie place, and can give a creepy feeling as you drive through it. Cisco began as a railroad town. It became a much-needed watering stop for the Denver and Rio Grande Western Railroad's steam engines in the 1880s. Sure, there were seasonal rains that watered the fields. However, the vast majority of the water for the area first had to be hauled in, and later piped in, from the nearby Colorado River.

Henry Ford's invention gave life to Cisco. After World War II, more and more Americans began to travel by automobile. Cisco was a welcoming haven for thirsty travelers headed through the arid desert. The town was situated on the main highway through the region at the time (US 6/50). A number of businesses sprouted up to serve those passing through, including restaurants, gas stations, and saloons. In the 1940s the town was home to about 200 people.

Slowly, a town grew up around the railroad station that primarily supported the nearby cattle ranchers and sheep herders. At the turn of the century, over 100,000 head of sheep were sheared here before being shipped to market. Cisco was a bustling ranching community during this time period.

In 1924, oil and natural gas were discovered in the region which gave a boost to the town. At one time, Cisco was the largest producer of oil and natural gas in the state.

Cisco began to decline in the 1950s. The railroad began to use diesel engines, replacing the coal-powered steam engines. The need for water stops diminished. Despite these setbacks, the town held on. Soon, something else came to its rescue: the discovery of uranium and vanadium in the area. They drew prospectors by the thousands. Cisco catered to the desert prospectors for several years, until the mining "craze" fizzled and the prospectors moved on.

Twenty years later, however, Highway I-70 came through, bypassing Cisco and its businesses. The economy immediately declined and people moved away. That was the end of Cisco.

## What It Is Like Today

Today, Cisco is a true ghost town, exuding almost an eerie feeling as you drive past it. There are many abandoned buildings and businesses, sitting amongst old railroad and oilfield junk and dozens of rusting cars.

# Remaining Buildings

Scattered ruins of old buildings remain. There is an abandoned gas station. The Cisco Landing Store appears to have been the last operating store in the ghost town and still stands. There is a fairly restored old cabin.

# How to Get There

Lies on U.S. Highway 6, south of I-70 near the Colorado border. Cisco is 50 miles east of Green River.

## Juicy Piece of History

One of the last businesses to survive in Cisco was a gas station and restaurant combined into one. One interesting story stands out. A biker had stopped for gas and took off without paying. The owner shot him. The gas station owner was then jailed, leaving the business to be run by his wife. It is said that the wife would only serve those whom she felt like serving, with the door kept closed and customers having to knock to get in. If she opened the door, a big dog would often bite the ankle of the customer. Anyone who was unfriendly towards the dog was not served. However, if they stayed calm, they would be allowed to purchase a meal.

# 56

# Mammoth

## History

In February 1870, a group of prospectors were examining outcrops in Juab County, when they made the big strike. Their find was high-grade silver. One of the prospectors shouted, "Boys. We've got ourselves a mammoth mine!" Other miners hurried to the new diggings, and before the month was out, a rough camp of tents and shacks grew up near the mines. By summer, the new camp had four hotels, several saloons, and a population of 2,500.

Originally staked in 1871, it remained unworked for two years due to the inhospitable combination of Indians, dry weather, and barren country. Mines in the area around Mammoth produced ore, silver, and gold. Miners rushed in and began a boomtown. The area was remote and the environment harsh; no water was to be found nearby. The miners piped in water for industrial use, but residents had to buy drinking water for ten cents a gallon.

Activity in Mammoth peaked around 1900–1910. Mammoth was officially incorporated in 1910, but began to decline soon after. By 1930, the population was down to 750, and the town was disincorporated.

## What It Is Like Today

Today, some residents still consider Mammoth home. There is some smaller scale mining that goes on in the area today for metals.

## Remaining Buildings

A few scattered remains exist.

## How To Get There

Mammoth is a semi-ghost town in northeastern Juab County, about three miles southeast of Eureka.

# Juicy Piece of History

Not every day could the pioneers say: "With a bunch of cows the McIntyres made two million." The fortune was not in milk but a mine called the Mammoth. The mine owners were Charles Crimson and partners, who were looking for investors. Crimson saw an opportunity to unload his share on the McIntyre Brothers who they considered to be gullible.

Sam and William McIntyre were driving a herd of Texas Longhorn cattle to market at Salt Lake City and were searching for good range land. They happen to bump into Crimson. The brothers were impressed with the mine owner's flattering description of the wealth that awaited some lucky man who would buy the Mammoth, invest some money in it, and sink the main shaft to the point where it would meet with a lode of silver.

Sam and William decided to trade their cattle for the biggest share of the mine. They spent some money developing the property and sank the shaft deeper. Lo and behold, just as their friend had predicted, they met up with the silver vein.

The Mammoth Mine did well. The McIntyres had built 22 furnace smelters and Sam had constructed a mansion, a fine brick home in the town of 1,000 people.

When the richest ores were exhausted and the poorer ones failed to pay the milling and smelting costs, the mills closed down and the people began to move away. Even the Mammoth operations ceased and Sam left his brick house to wandering cowboys and sheepherders.

# 57

# National

## History

Though coal was discovered in the area in 1908, a town wasn't developed until the National Coal Company began operations in 1926, naming the settlement after the company. Miners rushed to National to get in on the high wages being paid by the National Coal Company. Naturally the town they helped build was named National.

All of the houses and buildings were constructed of the same red brick. The mining company buildings and officials' homes were the only dwellings with indoor plumbing.

Coal was mined right up until the depression when the town was hard hit and died. The National Coal Company discontinued its operations in July 1938, and by the end of the year was sold under foreclosure. Though mining operations were continued once again by the new owner of the property, they were short lived and the town soon died permanently.

## What It Is Like Today

Today, a few foundations and crumbling buildings can still be spied along Gordon Creek.

## Remaining Buildings

A few scattered buildings remain. There is a large stone foundation across the creek which may be the remains of a railroad trestle.

## How To Get There

National is 3 miles from Coal City. Turn off US-6/191 onto Consumers Road, north of Price.

## Juicy Piece of History

The town shared a post office, school house, hospital, and amusement hall with the nearby mining camps of Consumers and Sweets, but had its own store and a central well. During the late 1920s, National grew by leaps and bounds, but by the 1930s, like other coal towns, National felt the sting of the depression.

# 58

# Newhouse

## History

The Cactus Mine was first identified as a silver mine in 1870. A succession of companies over the next thirty years failed to profit from the mine. Everything changed in 1900, when Samuel Newhouse bought the property. Samuel Newhouse was fresh from financial successes in Bingham Canyon. He had investments in England and France. Newhouse had a dream. He wanted to establish a model city for his miners and their families. The mining camp that formed on his land was initially known as Tent Town, for the temporary nature of its dwellings.

Under Newhouse's management, the silver mining business began to boom. He built over seventy stucco company houses for miners to rent. By 1905, the town, now named Newhouse, had many permanent structures, including a restaurant, library, livery stable, hospital, stores, hotel, opera house, and dance hall.

The company piped water five miles from the Wah Wah Springs and installed an electrical generation system. A town park was irrigated with excess water left over from mining and cooking purposes. Mr. Newhouse named town businesses after the mine: Cactus Trading Company, Cactus Club, Cactus Dancehall, and Cactus Cafe. There was a clubhouse at the center of his model city, containing a well-stocked library, pool tables, and a small bar. But it was a very proper place, for no drunks were allowed. Newhouse was a place of law and order.

The residents built an opera house and a dance hall. The excess water not used for mining, and culinary purposes were put to use irrigating the city park. The town even promoted prize fighting.

Newhouse wanted the town to be disciplined and family-friendly. Public drunkenness was strictly forbidden, and the only saloon permitted was built a mile from town, off of Newhouse's property. Mr. Newhouse offered a $50 prize to the first parents to have a baby in Newhouse, and he gave all the town's children Christmas presents.

Samuel Newhouse died before the completion of his dream, but his brother, Matt Newhouse, continued his legacy. In 1914, the Cactus Mill was torn down and most of the people moved away. Most of the miners took their families elsewhere. Many buildings, including the well-built dance hall, were moved thirty miles away to Milford. The cafe kept operating, serving those few miners who stayed on, until 1921 when it burned down.

## What It Is Like Today

There are some remaining buildings today.

# Remaining Buildings

Dozens of ruined buildings, foundations, and rubble remain at the town site, along with a row of old charcoal kilns.

# How To Get There

Located on the eastern edge of the Wah Wah Valley in Beaver County, and 5 miles from Frisco.

## Juicy Piece of History

Samuel Newhouse, who would become one of Utah's wealthiest mining magnates, was a lawyer from New York City. He moved to Leadville, Colorado, in 1879. At Leadville, Colorado, he was involved in the freighting business, and in 1883, he married Ida Stingley, a sixteen-year-old girl whose mother ran a boarding house in the town. The Newhouses operated a hotel in Leadville, and then Samuel acquired mining property at Ouray, Colorado, which he eventually sold for several million dollars.

While his wife preferred living outside of Utah, Samuel Newhouse's choice was Salt Lake City. In 1907, he launched a significant building program in the city designed to shift the city's center from the Temple Square area south four blocks to Exchange Place between 300 and 400 South Streets and between Main and State Streets. In 1907, construction began on the city's first skyscrapers, the Boston and the Newhouse buildings. Exchange Place was to be a little "Wall Street" with a grand hotel, named the Newhouse Hotel constructed between 1909 and 1915.

Newhouse owned four residences: a home at 175 East South Temple in Salt Lake City which he renovated as a colonial-style mansion in about 1905, an estate on Long Island, a chateau outside Paris, France, and a mansion in London, England. Over-extension ultimately proved Newhouse's financial downfall. The money from his mines could not finance his elaborate projects and World War I made it almost impossible to obtain loans from eastern U.S. and European sources. In 1914, Samuel and Ida separated. The South Temple mansion was sold, and between 1915 and 1919 Samuel resided at the Newhouse Hotel. He then sold his interest in the hotel and left for France, where he lived with his sister at the chateau outside Paris he had given to her. He died there on September 22, 1930 at the age of seventy-six.

# 59

# Ophir

## History

In 1865, Colonel Patrick E. Connor's far-ranging troops heard about the silver and soldiers of the U.S. Army discovering the area of Ophir. They noticed that Indians in the territory were using bullets made from silver. The soldiers soon found the source and proceeded to dispatch the Indians. They named the location St. Louis at first.

The Ophir Mine is linked to George Hearst, who came from humble beginnings in Missouri, but wound up being a millionaire. Hearst was always on the lookout for rich finds. He bought a one-sixth interest in the Ophir Mine. The Ophir mine began to produce in a big way.

Senator W.A. Clark of Montana owned mining properties at Ophir, and built a railroad. Ore from Ophir's mines were shipped to Godbe Smelter and the Walker Brothers Pioneer Mill at Martinsville. Most of the mineral was lead, silver, and zinc, with copper impurities and very little gold. A town sprang up and mining began in earnest. One of the old Bible-reading prospectors thought of King Solomon's mines, in the land of Ophir, saw a resemblance here, and the town was named. In 1870, it was officially named Ophir after the rich mines of King Solomon.

Like hundreds of boom towns across the West, rough board small shacks appeared as soon as the surveyor had stepped away from the plat. There were the typical mining town-saloons, gambling and dance halls, red-light houses, hotels, cafes, stores, and living quarters, all lining the narrow street at the bottom of the canyon. During its heyday, a number of ornamental homes and buildings were constructed.. Soon, the entire region was referred to as the "Comstock Lode."

Attracted to Ophir were those whose business was to pick the miners clean – gamblers, harlots, legitimate businessmen, and the usual array of gunmen. The town attracted thousands of miners from throughout the West who were disgruntled with their present lot and came to participate in the treasure hunt. By 1871, Ophir's population had reached 1,200.

The easy-going success of Ophir's affairs inspired some fancy stone and brick houses. Yet, its life proved shorter than many camps, for although its ore veins were rich, they were shallow. Except for a few big producers, like the Ophir Hill Mine, they were soon worked out.

In 1880, the boom was over. Most of the boomers and camp followers had melted away, leaving only fifty some odd miners, families, and a few merchants. There was still wealth in the canyon but it was much harder to extract than before.

By 1918, Ophir still had a post office, weekly newspaper, general store, daily stage line, railroad, and a population of 560. In 1930, a large flotation mill was built at the mouth of the canyon to reprocess the old tailings.

## What It Is Like Today

Old abandoned stores sit atop the hill coming into town. There are some current residents living here today.

## Remaining Buildings

Dozens of old buildings line the streets. The old stone post office still stands. Up off the main street is the old deserted school and several other abandoned houses and shops. There is also a cemetery on the hill.

## How To Get There

3.5 miles off State Highway 73; 4.5 miles east of State Highway 36.

## Juicy Piece of History

Born near Sullivan, Missouri, on September 3, 1820, to John and Elizabeth Collins Hearst, George was the oldest of three children. Although Hearst was said to have had a lifelong interest in books, he had only rudimentary reading abilities.

When George was 26, his father, William Hearst, died owing some $10,000 to his creditors. George immediately took on the responsibility for caring for his mother, younger sister, and crippled brother.

Before long, George had improved on the farm's profitability, opened a small store

and leased a couple of prospective lead mines. Within two years, he was able to pay off his father's debt.

It seemed that everything Hearst touched literally turned to gold. In 1880, George acquired the small *San Francisco Examiner* as repayment for a gambling debt. *The Examiner*, would later become the foundation of the Hearst Publishing Empire. He became a millionaire and a very successful man.

Hearst bought a share of the Ophir Mine and made the town prosper.

# 60
# Sego Canyon

## History

Sego got its start in the early 1890s when an affluent farmer/rancher named Harry Ballard discovered coal on land adjacent to his ranch. Keeping his discovery a secret, he began to buy the adjacent property and started coal operations on a small scale.

The coal was initially dug out manually and hauled down the narrow canyon by wagons. Soon, news of the high quality coal in Sego Canyon reached Salt Lake City. When a hardware store owner named B.F. Bauer heard of the find, he bought out Ballard's property and formed the American Fuel Company.

In 1911, the company began to develop the area with grand plans for long-term coal production. They built the American Fuel Company Store, a boarding house, mining buildings, the first coal washer west of the Mississippi River, and a tipple. They also renamed the settlement Neslin, for the general manager of the American Fuel Company, Richard Neslin.

By 1916, primary investor, B.F. Bauer, was not happy with the low profits and fired the general manager, Richard Neslin. The town's name was then renamed Sego, for the state flower of Utah.

In camps like Sego, miners drank and whored and gambled and murdered. They worked close to danger and lived right on the edge of it.

In 1947, the mine was ordered closed and the property offered for sale at a Sheriff's auction in Moab. By that time, only twenty-seven miners were employed, many of whom had worked at the mine for decades and were devastated. The remaining miners agreed to pool their money and make bid. They were successful when they were able to purchase the equipment and property for $30,010. They changed the name to the Utah Grand Coal Company and once again began operations. However, tragedy struck in 1949, when a fire burned the tipple, drastically decreasing production. That same year, the railroad ceased operations to Sego, which required the new company to purchase dump trucks, and loading ramps, as well as building a new tipple. However, the employee-owned company persevered and recovered. They were adamant to keep it going.

There was nothing they could do about the final blow, when in the early 1950s, the railroad began to use diesel engines, replacing the coal powered steam engines and reducing the need for the mine's products. Sego became an official ghost town.

## What It Is Like Today

Today, the old site continues to display numerous signs of its prosperous past. The stone walls of the old American Fuel Company Store continue to stand, though its windows and roof are long gone. Nearby, are the walls of another stone building, as well as the two-story, crumbling wood "American" boarding house.

## Remaining Buildings

Throughout the canyon can be found numerous other crumbling structures, mine shafts, foundations, and the old railroad bridges that crossed the creek. The cemetery provides an overgrown look at the past in its few marked and unmarked headstones.

## How To Get There

The drive into the canyon requires a high clearance vehicle and should never be attempted if storms are expected, as flash floods are common. The exit to Sego Canyon is 25 miles east of Green River on I-70.

### Juicy Piece of History

Sego provides not only a peek at prehistoric rock-art, but also the remains of the old coal town of Sego, a once thriving coal mining camp.

On Sego Canyon Road, are the petroglyphs and pictographs left by several different cultures.

The strangest thing about Sego's mines were the dinosaur tracks found at many places in the coal beds.

# 61

# Silver Reef

## History

In 1874, a man named William T. Barbee was credited with getting the mining going. In 1875, he had twenty-two claims here. In 1876, the area became an established town. Barbee quickly set up a town and called it Bonanza City. There wasn't much to Bonanza City, but the property values were high anyway. Most of the miners could not afford property there, so they set up a tent city in a rocky section of land and named it "Rockpile." It was aptly named because at that time a rock pile with tents is exactly what it was. The town changed the name of "Rockpile" to Silver Reef.

Main Street was over a mile long. The town's population advanced to over 1,500 during the peak years. There were six mills in operation. There were hotels, stores, saloons, a bank, several restaurants, a hospital, dance halls, newspapers, a Chinatown and three cemeteries. Within no time, the town boasted more than 100 businesses stretched out along a mile long main street, including nine grocery stores, six saloons, and a newspaper called the *Silver Echo*. There were also eight dry goods stores, a Wells Fargo office, hotels, boarding houses, and five restaurants. The grocery stores outnumbered the saloons.

Chinese laborers fresh off the railroad work drifted into Silver Reef, setting up their own Chinatown.

Though surrounded by Mormon settlements, Silver Reef never had a Mormon Church; rather, the Catholic Church was the only one in town, a building they allowed the Presbyterians to use for services. A school was also used by other denominations for services. Here, the community also held public meetings and celebrations. The town maintained a race track during its prosperous years where visitors from St. George gathered with their blooded horses raced in the region.

Silver Reef experienced the usual murders expected in an unrestricted mining camp. In 1880, a union organizer named Tom Forrest killed Mike Corbis, a popular mine foreman. He was jailed for his protection from angry miners at Silver Reef. On the day of their friend's funeral, the miners went to St. George and dragged Forrest from his jail cell. He was hung without a trial from a tree in front of George Cottom's house. After watching the hanging, Cottom, an old Mormon, who didn't like anything about Silver Reef, said, "I have observed that tree growing there for the last twenty-five years. This is the first time I have ever seen it bearing fruit."

By 1880, Wells Fargo had shipped more than $8,000,000 worth of bouillon from Silver Reef's mines. Things, however, were beginning to change.

Demise was on its way. Three factors came into play in 1881 to bring the end of the boom. First, the world silver market dropped. Second, the mines filled with water faster than it could be pumped out. And, finally, the mine stockholders lowered the miners' wages. Miners could not afford to stay. Most of the mines were closed by 1884 and the town died.

By 1890, less than 200 people remained in the area and the following year, the last mine shut down, though ore continued to be brought out of the area for the next decade. In the early 1900s, many of the remaining buildings were demolished, and in 1908, a fire destroyed most of what was left.

## What It Is Like Today

Today, a number of summer cabins or "rural retreat" homes lie just north of the town site. Scattered around the town are numerous abandoned ruins and foundations, especially in the gully behind the old town site, where crumbling mine buildings continue to stand. Nearby are the remains of both a Catholic and a Protestant cemetery.

## Remaining Buildings

The 1877 Wells Fargo Office was utilized as a residence until the late 1940s. Listed on the National Register of Historic Places, today it serves as a museum and art gallery. Behind the Wells Fargo building is a restored powder house that serves as an information center.

## How To Get There

Silver Reef is about 15 miles northeast of St. George, Utah just off Highway 15.

## Juicy Piece of History

There are many stories as to how the town was discovered. The most often told tale is about a prospector named John Kemple who had been roaming the sandstone reefs in search of any metallic color back in 1866. The lone prospector was wandering over the bleak ridges searching for metallic color, sure the sandstone reefs which stretched everywhere were hopeless, yet he had to keep moving because it was intensely cold and night was coming on. He was tired and chilled.

Kemple reached the Mormon settlement of Leeds after dark but a cheerfully glowing lamp in a window led him to a hospitable family who made him welcome and threw more fuel on the fireplace blaze. As Kemple sat staring into the fire, he allegedly saw a small shining stream ooze from an overheated rock. He caught the drops and later confirmed his belief they were silver.

The next day, he then began to search for the source of what he believed was silver. Though he did find a small sample, it wasn't enough to keep him in the area and he soon moved on to Nevada.

In 1874, John Kemple returned to the area and established the Harrisburg Mining District. Kemple located many claims but never developed them.

(By 1875 there were many prospectors in the area.)

# 62

# Thompson Springs

## History

The town began when E.W. Thompson, who lived near the springs, operated a sawmill to the north, near the Book Cliffs. The area was named "Thompson's" after the original owner, E.W. Thompson. Soon a small community grew up, made up of small-scale farmers, sheepherders, and cattlemen.

Sometime later, Harry Ballard discovered a large vein of coal on land adjacent to his ranch about five miles north of Thompson's. Keeping his discovery quiet, he soon bought the surrounding property and started coal operations on a small scale.

Before long, he owned a hotel, store, saloon, and several homes in the small settlement. However, Ballard sold his operation to Salt Lake City investors in 1911, and the coal mining town was born, bringing more prosperity to the area.

A post office was established in 1890. Soon, the little community was large enough to convince the Denver and Rio Grande Western Railroad to add a railroad stop in the settlement. Cattle and sheep men welcomed the railroad, which soon became a small shipping point for their stock.

In the meantime, commercial mining was progressing rapidly, bringing out numerous loads of high-grade coal. Though the coal was in high demand; the mine suffered financial difficulties from the start, due to lack of water and management issues. Railroad operations to the mine ceased in 1949, which placed further operational issues on the mine. However, the mine continued in Sego Canyon until 1955, when the railroad began to use diesel engines. The diesel engines replaced the coal powered steam engines and reduced the need for the mine's products.

Another blow was dealt to Thompson when I-70 was built through the area in the 1970s. Thompson had survived the mining decline, as it was situated on a main highway through the area, NV-128, and provided services to travelers passing through the region.

However, when the interstate was developed, the town found itself just a few miles north of the new highway and traffic through the small community dramatically decreased and businesses began to close.

## What It Is Like Today

A few remaining buildings can be seen.

## Remaining Buildings

Though an exit still exists from I-70 into the town, it is a bit off the interstate, and its businesses are all closed.

## How To Get There

Off the Interstate of I-70.

### Juicy Piece of History

Thompson became important in 1914, when the Ballard and Thompson Railroad was constructed from the mines at Sego to connect at the Thompson railhead.

Though the town never grew very large, it contained two motels, a saloon, the railroad station, a couple of stores, a school, a restaurant, and a number of homes.

# 63

# Topaz

## History

The Topaz War Relocation Center, also known as the Central Utah Relocation Center (Topaz), was a camp which housed Japanese descent and immigrants who had come to the United States from Japan. While many of the older generation were from Japan, most of those under 30 years of age were *Nisei*, first-generation American citizens of Japanese descent, and *Kibei*, Nisei who had been sent to Japan as children for periods of traditional schooling.

In February 1942, President Franklin D. Roosevelt issued Executive Order 9066 which mandated that the roughly 120,000 Americans of Japanese descent, the vast majority of whom lived along the West Coast, be taken inland to internment camps where they could remain under guard and suspicion until the war ended. Military thinking was that the Americans of Japanese ancestry, and most of them were actually U.S. citizens, posed a threat to national security. First housed in places such as racetrack stables, eventually they were moved to various camps, hundreds or even thousands of miles from home.

In March, authorities began rounding them up, often with little or no warning, and took them to temporary holding camps while permanent facilities were found and developed. Most were business owners, shop keepers, artists, and architects. At Topaz, out of necessity, they became farmers, but they also had a lot of time to read, paint, and draw.

The U.S. built ten permanent residential facilities: two in California, two in Arizona, one each in Idaho, California, and Wyoming, two in Arkansas and Topaz in Utah.

The camp consisted of 19,800 acres (8,012.8 ha). The well-planned town consisted of 42 city blocks with 12 military-type barrack buildings on each block. There was also a large 128-bed hospital, a theatre, 5 churches, a recreation hall and even a newspaper named *Topaz Times*. Most Topaz internees lived in the central residential area located approximately 15 miles (24.1 km) west of Delta, though some lived as caretakers overseeing agricultural land and areas used for light industry and animal husbandry.

Surrounded by desert, Topaz was an entirely new environment for internees. At an altitude of 4,600 feet (1,402.1 m) above sea level, arid and subject to dust storms and wide temperatures swung during night and day.

Topaz was opened September 11, 1942, and eventually became the fifth-largest city in Utah, with over 9,000 internees and staff. It was closed on October 31, 1945.

Internees in all of the camps left their mark on many of the improvements made during their imprisonment. Names, comments, and even poetry were impressed into drying concrete in a number of projects, some in English and others in Japanese. These can be seen today, though visitors must search for them on their own.

While a cemetery site was dedicated, there is no record that it was ever used. Internees' bodies were transported 150 miles (241.4 km) to Salt Lake City, cremated, and returned to their families so that they could be taken when they left Topaz.

Also in the camp were stores, cold-drink shops, barber and beauty shops. Periodically, they were permitted to travel to Delta to shop. To meet demand, Delta even had a fresh fish shop during this time.

The number of Japanese confined in Topaz reached 8,778. Not long after Topaz was established, authorities realized that there was no need to confine most of the people who had been brought there, because nearly all were loyal American citizens. They were allowed to return home. But while living in Topaz, the so-called prisoners were allowed to roam the desert, prospecting or searching for Topaz crystals.

As mentioned, Topaz was closed in 1945. Contracts were given to salvage everything, as if to erase the shameful blot from the desert's face. The job was done so well that practically nothing remains to show that people once lived there.

The Topaz Museum reminds visitors of the importance of preserving the rights of the minority. It is up to the majority to do this. The site is a U.S. National Historic Landmark.

# What It Is Like Today

Topaz has remaining buildings. A visit to the Topaz Museum is a must.

# Remaining Buildings

Some foundations can be seen.

# How To Get There

Located in central Juab County north of Delta and 20 miles south of Topaz Mountain.

# Juicy Piece of History

The internment of Americans of Japanese ancestry during WWII was one of the worst violations of civil rights in the history of the United States. The government and the US Army, citing "military necessity," locked up over 110,000 men, women, and children in 10 remote camps. These Americans were never convicted or even charged with any crime, yet were incarcerated for up to 4 years in prison camps surrounded by barbed wire and armed guards.

One internee, Dave Tatsuno (1913-2006), had a movie camera smuggled into the camp, at the urging of his supervisor, Walter Honderick. A film which he shot from 1943 to 1945 became the documentary *Topaz*. This film was deemed "culturally significant" by the United States Library of Congress in 1997, and was the second film to be selected for preservation in the National Film Registry (behind the *Zapruder* film of the JFK assassination). Until his death, Tatsuno was an Emeritus member of the board of the Topaz Museum, which is working to preserve the site.

# Bibliography

Aspen Historical Society, *Aspen's Early Days: Walking Tour*, Johnson Publishing, Boulder Colorado, 1975

Blari, Edward, and Churchill, Richard E., *Everybody Came to Leadville*, B & B Printers, 1977

Brown, Georgina, *Victorian Nostalgia: A Look at Leadville's Homes of Fortune*, B & B Printers, Gunnison, CO, 1976

Feitz, Leland, *A Quick History of Victor: Colorado's City of Mines*, Little London Press, Colorado Springs, 1969

Houze, Lynn Johnson, *Images of America: Cody*, Arcadia Publishing, California, 2008

League of Women Voters of Aspen/Pitkin County, *Aspen: People, Places and Things*, Aspen, CO, 1981

Luders, Mary, Ed., *The Smithsonian Guides to Historic America: Rocky Mountain States*, Stewart, Tabori, & Chang publishers, NY, 1998

Miller, Donald, *Ghost Towns of Wyoming*, Pruett Publishing, Colorado, 1972

Moulton, Candy, *Roadside History to Wyoming*, Mountain Press Publishing Company, Montana, 1995

O Neill, Zora, *Santa Fe, Taos, & Albuquerque*, Moon Guidebooks, Avalon Travel Publishing, CA, 2006

Pence, Mary Lou, and Lola M. Homsher, *The Ghost Towns of Wyoming*, Hasting House Publishers, New York, 1956

Pearce, Sarah J., and Eflin, Roxanne, *Guide to Historic Aspen and the Roaring Fork Valley*, Cordillera Press Inc., 1990

Southworth, Dave, *Colorado Mining Camps*, Wild Horse Publishing, 1997

Thompson, George A, *Some Dreams Die: Utah's Ghost Towns and Lost Treasures*, Dream Garden Press, Salt Lake City, Utah, 1982

Varney, Philip, *Arizona's Best Ghost Towns, A Practical Guide by Philip Varney*, Northland Press, Flagstaff, AZ, 1980

Voynick Stephen M., *Leadville: A Miner's Epic*, Mountain Press Publishing Company, Missoula, 1984

Weir, Darlene Godat, *Leadville's Ice Palace: A Colossus in the Colorado Rockies*, Gilliland Printing Inc., Kansas, 1994

Weiser, Kathy, Editor, *Legends of America*, www.legendsofamerica.com